# Chocolate Unw

*The Politics of Pleasure*

# Cat Cox

## The Women's Environmental Network

**Cat Cox** obtained a degree in Pharmacology from the University of London and has worked for the Women's Environmental Network (WEN) for nearly three years. She has contributed to the Open University 1991/92 Women's Studies Course Book and is co-author of *A Tissue of Lies: Disposable Paper and the Environment*. In writing a briefing paper for WEN on *Ecofeminism* , she encapsulated the philosophy which guides many women's groups around the world to work in both a spiritual and practical way towards redressing the balance of a polluted planet. She has spoken and facilitated workshops on issues relating to women and the environment and has travelled extensively throughout Asia and America, and has also worked in Australia and Japan.

**The Women's Environmental Network (WEN)** was formed in 1988 and aims to empower, inform and educate women who care about the environment. One of Britain's leading environmental pressure groups, WEN has successfully campaigned on issues such as the environmental and health effects of disposable sanitary protection, the overpackaging of consumer goods and the destruction of old-growth temperate rainforest for one-use paper products. WEN has over 2,500 individual members, represents a network of over 200 organisations and is part of an international network of groups working on issues relating to women and the environment. Previously published books include *The Sanitary Protection Scandal* and *A Tissue of Lies; Disposable Paper and the Environment.*
**For more details contact WEN, Aberdeen Studios, 22 Highbury Grove, London N5 2EA    Tel: 071 354 8823**

# Acknowledgements

I would like to extend my thanks to all those individuals and organisations who have provided research material, input and help with this book, for the production of a piece of work such as this is not feasible without the assistance and support of a great many people.

I would especially like to thank Barbara Dinham for her help during the research and on the final draft, and similarly thanks must go to Tim Lang for his comments. Thanks also to Peter Madden for his comments on the final body of work. I would like to thank Paul Elshof at SOMO, Dirk de Jager at TIE, and Marijke Mooy at Inzet in Amsterdam. I would further like to thank all those people who assisted me with research in Malaysia, in particular Carolyn Marr in Penang, Rajoo and Coral at SAM Kuala Lumpur and also Sarojini Rengam and Vasanthi Arumugam of PAN Asia and the Pacific; also James Lockheed and Prema at SIMBA for making available further information on this region. Thanks also to individuals for help on the other regions, including Patrick Aculey and Charles Abugre who provided information on Ghana, and Carlinhos on Brazil. Thanks must go to Sue Dibb at the London Food Commission and Dr. Alistair Hay at Leeds University, also to Eric Millstone for assistance with additives and Dr Charlie Clutterbuck for casting his expert eye over the final text on pesticide residues. Thanks to Mary Jane Rust at The Women's Therapy Centre for sharing her views on women, food and chocolate and to members of government and industry for their response to requests for information.

This work could not have been completed without the help of the women at WEN who have assisted with research, critique, and support. I would particularly like to thank Jo McAndrews, Lynette Samara Green and Shara Beral, also Rebekah Rowles, Marian Connolly and Laura Canning for their research work, and Hilary Flenley for providing the index. Thanks to Naomi Diamond for her valuable contribution to research and her overall support and I would also especially like to thank Julie Cook, Helen O'Hara, and Vicki Carroll, together with Ann Link, Helen Moss, Kirsty Burns, Rebecca Rees, Lin Collins and Clare Flenley for practical support, editing and constructive criticism. Thank you to Jocelyn Lucas for her superb design and illustrations. Not least

I want to thank Bernadette Vallely for offering the challenge to write this book in the first instance and her help in bringing it to completion. And finally I would like to thank Katrina Amos, who with skill and steadfast commitment has been invaluable in facilitating the quality and flow of this work.

# Chocolate Unwrapped
## The Politics of Pleasure

## Introduction

*Myths*

### 1 Sanctity     10
*Cocoa and Sacred Rites*
*Early European Influences*
*Mass Consumption*

### 2 Passion     18
*Sexual Images*
*Chemicals in the Body*
*Advertising Myths*

### 3 Pleasure     26
*The Chocoholic*
*Dieting, Binging and Battles*
*Beauty and Guilt*

### 4 Goodness     34
*A Healthy Food?*
*Additives*
*Health Effects*
*Fat and Sugar in our Diet*

### 5 Purity     44
*Pre-packaged Pesticides*
*Residue Testing*
*Body Intakes and Acceptable Doses*
*Pesticides and our Children*
*Circle of Poison*

**Chocolate Unwrapped** The Politics of Pleasure

*Realities*

**6 Land** 58
*West Africa* 60
The Arrival of a Cash Crop
A Quality Product
Political and Economic Changes
The World Bank, IMF and SAPs
Social Implications
The Paradox of Debt

*Brazil* 70
Industrial Development
Working Conditions
The Oppression of Women
The Influence of Transnationals

*Malaysia* 78
Life on the Plantation
Economic Expansion
Opening up the Land
Resettlement into a Cash Economy

*Indonesia* 88
Transmigration
Development of Plantations
The Threat to Diversity

**7 Pesticides** 96
*Monoculture*
Pesticides Used on Cocoa
Malaysia
Paraquat
Brazil
Ghana
Lindane
Dangers in Production
The Pesticide Trade

**8 Profit** 112
*Commodity Trading*
Cocoa Agreements
The Processing Industry
Concentration of the Manufacturers
New Markets

*Alternatives*

## 9  Biotechnology　126
*Improving the Bean*
*Creating In-built Resistance*
*Manipulating the Cocoa Plant*
*Effects on Producers*
*Searching for Substitutes*
*The Redundant Cocoa Tree*


## 10  Conscious Consumption　138
*Fair Trade*
*Organic*
*Medium-term Strategies*
*Long-term Strategies*


## References　148


## Appendices
*Pesticides Health & Environmental Effects*　169
*Company Profiles*　180
*Tables*　187

To women's courage, women's vision and women's hope.

# Introduction

The simple chocolate bar has come a long way from its earliest incarnation in arcane ceremonies in the Middle Americas. Today, it highlights the inequities of an economic and trading system which promotes unlimited consumerism, encourages environmentally damaging development and impoverishes people worldwide.

Modern chocolate eating habits are fuelled by an industry which must continually expand sales in order to survive. Chocolate consumption has continued to rise in the traditional markets of Europe and North America for over a century but, as consumers in Europe reach saturation point, manufacturers are looking for new markets. They are expanding their manufacturing, distribution and sales operations to cultures and climates from East Europe to South East Asia, fuelling worldwide consumption but benefiting few beyond the industry itself.

Chocolate is the major binge food and as such highlights the apparent contradictions of women's relationship with food unique to Western culture, where millions of women are experiencing eating disorders. With one woman in 50 in England suffering from bulimia, one woman in five binging once a month and 90% of women having been on slimming diets[1], the extent of disordered eating patterns affects women on a scale thought inconceivable a decade ago and indicates an experience of chocolate consumption at variance with the myth portrayed in popular culture.

Women are the biggest consumers of chocolate. Sold to women with images of sensuality and indulgence, multi-million pound advertising campaigns by the manufacturers encourage us to consume a product which is bought mostly on impulse and chocolate sales increase annually. Chocolate consumption may induce guilt and anxiety as a fattening food, yet it is a stark irony that it is promoted by women who are icons of contemporary beauty. For, where women have learnt that value is culturally bestowed on beauty, where to be thin is to be beautiful and to be beautiful is to be valued, body image has assumed enormous cultural importance, and the drive to meet the contemporary representation of beauty is overwhelming. Chocolate highlights the less visible cultural oppression of women in Western culture, in response to which women in the North are waging war on their bodies with food.

Grown in the developing regions of the South, the circumstances of production are unenviable. It is women who work predominantly on the cocoa plantations of Malaysia as pesticide sprayers, where working under ill-equipped conditions, agrochemical application has affected many women's health. Some estimates state that 25 million agricultural workers in the South suffer from the effects of pesticide poisoning each year.

Cocoa production has also disenfranchised the women who must sacrifice motherhood to get a job growing cocoa on the cocoa plantations of Brazil, where under highly inequitable conditions, women are increasingly required to become sterilized in order to get work. Throughout these regions women earn so little for their work that many are unlikely to have ever tasted chocolate. This is the other side of our experience of chocolate as consumers, where the realities of production entail oppressive and disempowering working conditions for the women and men who have limited options but to work to produce a cash crop. These women's experiences serve to temper our complacent consumption and demand examination of the politics and underlying paradigm which sanctions this situation.

Chocolate consumption is fuelled by a multi-billion pound industry which must continually expand sales in order to succeed. This is the nature of Western economics which is dependent upon consumption and is reflected in Western culture which promotes consumerism. Our desire for chocolate has been mediated and provoked as huge financial resources are put into advertising to encourage chocolate consumption in the traditional markets of Europe and North America. The British - the third biggest chocolate eaters in the world - spent over £2 billion on chocolate in 1992 and despite women's consternation, our chocolate eating habits continue to grow each year.

Over 1000 brands of chocolate are now on sale in the North, yet the majority of these products are produced by just five transnational corporations whose interests are global. It is the motivation of this industry which engineers the cycle of chocolate consumption, facilitating cheap snacks for consumers, and thereby entailing hardship and ill health for producers, whilst the companies accrue vast profits in between. Although powered by the industry, the cocoa chain is also motivated by a deep and pervasive cultural movement, as current Western values are exported globally as 'development'

Increased production of cocoa has been driven by the promise of development and the pressing need for countries in the South to earn foreign exchange. Global economic institutions recognise primary commodities as a major source of income from which Third World nations can repay debt. Individual governments and these institutions encouraged cocoa growers at a time when the price was high, but with short term vision and a rationale which failed to predict that the price would fall to the detriment of producers worldwide. Overall, the massive expansion of this cash crop has served few who are involved in its production whilst huge stocks of cheap beans have been built up in the warehouses of the traders and manufacturers of the North.

Independent smallholders currently receive little payment for their crops and are reverting to food production. Even under the most chemical intensive production on the Malaysian cocoa plantations, the income received no longer meets the costs incurred. Plantations are able to produce more cheaply than the smallholders. This is not just because they use chemical intensive methods of production, but also because they pay their workers so little in their drive to be competitive and profitable.

While the cocoa price has fallen, expansion has also incurred a high ecological cost. Massive expansion has been achieved by turning over more land to cash crops, by growing on plantations using large quantities of chemicals and by creating plants which are dependent upon chemical input. All these measures have led away from sustainable and environmentally benign techniques and exacerbated environmental degradation.

Through intensive agriculture, the land has been drenched with toxic pesticides and chemical fertilisers in order to maintain monoculture production. The ubiquitous use of these synthetic organic chemicals was worth around £15 million in sales in 1990. On the cocoa plantations of South East Asia, where agrochemicals are an intrinsic part of the production process, the crop simply cannot be grown in this monocultural manner without a heavy input of chemicals. Malaysian plantation owners, eager to supply European markets, consider that cocoa is not a viable crop otherwise.

Pesticides have polluted the land they were designed to make more fertile and have contaminated the food itself. Contamination of chocolate has been an inevitable outcome of the use of mass agrochemicals on the cocoa crop. Despite the findings that show pesticide residues do exist in the final product, manufacturers and governments alike assure us that such contamination of food is safe and normal. However, there can be no denying that pesticides are dangerous to the health of those whose job it is to apply the chemicals on the plantations and also contaminate the earth.

From cocoa production to chocolate consumption, the chocolate bar highlights the inequities of our contemporary cultural values. Economics promote short term profit-making strategy over long term sustainability in the drive to increase consumption. Reductionist scientific attitudes have concurred with capitalist endeavour to encourage activity with small regard for holistic ecological consequences. Patriarchal values have also contrived to degrade women for the sake of cheap labour to enhance productivity, whilst Western women are encouraged to consume a product they may not really want. In taking a product such as chocolate, wide-ranging perspectives are woven together - this is the nature of the holistic view presented here. Through examining both the everyday myths and the realities of wider experience, the process of change can be addressed.

# *Myths*

# Sanctity

*Cocoa and Sacred Rites*

The source of our fascination with chocolate lies in its mythic roots as a sacred and celebrated plant of the early civilisations in Central and South America. Chocolate is not a modern concoction - it has been around since antiquity. Its cultured origins arose in Central America, long before the European invaders and traders brought it across the Atlantic 500 years ago where it assumed a European identity.

Cocoa is a tree native to the tropical rainforest of Central and South America where it still grows wild amongst the remaining lush humid vegetation. The tree can be traced over 2000 years ago to the eastern slopes of the Andes from where it spread westward across to the rich Amazon basin and then northward to the rainforest of Central America. The stands of cocoa trees were sacred groves and the tree, with its offerings of dark rich beans, was revered by the native Amerindians. They believed that the cocoa beans originated in the spirit realms and were an offering from the gods. To the Mayans, whose culture flourished nearly 2000 years ago, cocoa had been the food of the gods and was one of the most important of the sacred plants upon which their culture was founded. A spiritual dimension pervaded all aspects of Mayan life and cocoa was portrayed as a symbol of fertility on the huge sculpted stone temples. Carved into sacred stone, cocoa pods appear growing on vines as symbols of life and being offered to the gods like the hearts of sacrificial victims[1] and the cocoa tree itself was protected by one of the pantheon of Earth Goddesses - Ixcacao[2].

Guided by spiritual observance and governed by a theocracy of priest kings, community life was punctuated by ritual, celebration, fasting and feasts that honoured the spiritual dimension of life and marked the passing of time. The highly stylised rituals, through which the people connected with the earth, involved incense, rites and offerings, and cocoa was used on these occasions both as a sacred offering of the beans and drunk as the concoction 'chocolatl'[3]. The Mayan priests were the originators of this process of making a rich, thick and bitter beverage from cocoa beans. After roasting over a fire, cocoa nibs released from inside the beans were crushed to form a powder and ground maize meal, vanilla, chilli, honey and flowers were added. This was the drink consumed at all ceremonies and drunk daily in the households of nobles and priests as a rite and a luxury.

Cocoa was valued not just as a symbol of sanctity, but also as a symbol of prosperity. Trade was vibrant at the height of the Central American civilisation with traders bringing goods from both the south and the north. Gold, silver, turquoise, obsidian, quetzal feathers, maize, oil, beans, cotton, shells and copal incense were carried long distances and exchanged in the market place. Cocoa was one of the most valued items of trade and the beans were imbued with such value that they were used as currency at a fixed market rate. Later in the region, one hundred cocoa beans were noted as the price of a slave. Today, cocoa beans are still sometimes offered as small change in the markets of southern Mexico[4].

It seems that, for the Mayans, spiritual significance was not lost in mercantile activity. For the Aztecs whose culture arose around 1200 AD, after the decline of the Mayan civilisation, cocoa also retained its sacred significance as well as its market value. It was from the Aztec civilisation that the marauding Spanish conquistadors first took sacks of cocoa beans and carried them over the Atlantic to Europe in the 1400s.   When Cortez landed in Mexico, he had met the Aztec ruler Moctezuma in the fabled city of Teotihuacan. He was believed to be their ancient god Quetzalcoatl, the white feathered warrior, the Lord of the Wind, prophesied to return to the land of the American people. Consequently, he was royally received and offered gifts of silver and gems and handed a chalice of gold containing chocolatl, the exotic drink of the Aztecs. To the Aztecs the latter was as valuable as their precious gold and silver metals.

Cocoa beans were collected as tribute from vanquished neighbouring peoples and used as currency for trade. For the Aztecs, it could also heal the mind and body and, through it, they could commune with their demanding and bloodthirsty gods. Fermented and roasted over a fire, these precious beans were crushed and mixed with spices and flowers, then drunk as in previous centuries both in ritual and in celebration. Moctezuma was reputed to have drunk 50 cups a day with a further 2000 jars of the beverage prepared for his court. This is the drink which Cortez received, to which he preferred to add milk and sugar, and which he then, along with gold and silver and the wealth of the Central American nations, took home to Spain as a luxurious indulgence, a cure-all and an aphrodisiac[5].

*Early European Influences*

Europeans have passed down these ancient tales of the fabled properties of the exotic beans through numerous generations, modifying them to match their cultural aspirations and commercial needs. The healing and aphrodisiac reputation of chocolate has appeared in all its transformations, from spiced ritual potion to hot milk chocolate drink and on to mass-produced milk chocolate bar. The sense of sanctity, however, was lost as cocoa was bought over the Atlantic by Spanish traders with eurocentric views and monotheistic faith. Indeed, chocolate drinking was banned in the newly founded Mexican churches by the Spanish missionaries because it provoked such uproar and high spirits amongst the Spanish and newly converted congregation. In the Spanish court, chocolate was a luxury of the nobility and was kept secret for over a century. It came out of seclusion on the Spanish peninsula when a Spanish princess arrived in the French court to marry Louis XIV in 1660 and brought it with her.

As it became popular throughout Europe, the image of luxury, healing and aphrodisiac properties spread with it. The Jacobean landed gentry of 17th-century London, who met to drink hot chocolate in luxurious chocolate houses in town, referred to the sensual and healing benefits of their expensive chocolate drinking habits in academic and literary texts of the time. In Britain, rather than a drink of the court, it was sold in specialist shops from the beginning. Café society flourished as chocolate houses became established throughout the capital. The most well known was the Cocoa Tree, famous in the days of Queen Anne. Originally it was the headquarters of the Jacobite party, then the Tories and then it flourished as a literary club frequented by poets, historians and socialites who came to indulge in this new, exotic and expensive habit. Cocoa was certainly considered something very special in those times - at 75p a pound and highly taxed by the government as a lucrative luxury, only the very wealthy could afford it[6].

Fuelled by the far reaching 18th-century capitalist notions of economics, growth and expansion and facilitated by 19th-century mechanical invention, our chocolate eating habits have undergone a phenomenal change. Invented in Holland by Van Houten, in the late 1800s, the cocoa press extracted cocoa butter out of the beans to leave cocoa powder. This was a revolutionary development. The ground powder made a smoother drink and the pressed butter, when combined with more cocoa powder and sugar, made the first bar of chocolate. The British firm Cadbury invested in the machine and brought it to the UK, where business boomed and chocolate, once an elite pastime, became an affordable and accessible treat. Cadbury made bars, blocks and boxes of chocolates; they put in sugary fruit centres and produced elaborate packaging designs. They sold in their thousands[7].

*Mass Consumption*

Today the various chocolate companies sell millions. The Nestlé-Rowntree Kit Kat plant makes 6.5 million Kit Kats every day[8]. Cadbury are rolling Wispa bars off the conveyor belt at a rate of over 1600 a minute[9]. Chocolate sales have been on the increase in Britain ever since the first grocer to stock cocoa powder, Mary Tuke, began in business in 1725 and chocolate had returned to the Americas, with the first recorded sale in a Boston apothecary in 1712. Today it is produced in the US in larger quantities than anywhere else in the world. Milton Hershey set up a chocolate manufacturing plant in Pennsylvania in 1905 to make Hershey bars and Forest E. Mars first made Mars bars in Chicago in the early 1930s. These two companies now account for half of the annual US$8 billion confectionery market[10]. As a product of mass manufacture and mass consumption, chocolate is now cheap, plentiful and available in every supermarket, garage and newsagent. Present in ever increasing quantities and in ever multiplying variations, the choice now extends to over 1000 brands. In the face of such availability, however, the earlier connotation of chocolate as a luxury has never quite slipped in the way products such as tea and coffee have come to be regarded as essential and mundane elements of the weekly shop.

The promotion of chocolate as a luxury, a sensual experience and a health food are rather extravagant associations to make of our 20th-century chocolate eating experience. Although little attention was ever paid to chocolate consumption as a religious rite in Europe, over half of all boxed chocolates are eaten at Christmas. Pre-Christmas television airtime runs chock-a-block with chocolate advertisements and the British merrily spend around £450 million on chocolate in our Christmas eating marathon[11].

Confectionery is a big seller; in fact, it outsells cereals, bread and milk with chocolate accounting for around two-thirds of the confectionery market (see Table 1). Half a million tonnes of chocolate was consumed in Britain in 1991, earning the industry over £2.5 billion, with Kit Kat, the biggest selling chocolate bar, earning over £100 million alone in sales in the same year. Women consume much more chocolate than men, annually buying as much as 66% and eating a much as 39% of all confectionery[12].

Easter has become another high spot for the chocolate industry and its importance is increasing. Over 80 million chocolate eggs were sold in the run up to Easter 1990, 20 million more than five years previously. The 'Easter bunny' is now best known for being moulded in chocolate but was once believed to lay the Easter eggs or hide them in the garden for children to search out. Children in Germany still search out eggs hidden by the 'Osterhase' on Easter morning. Originating as the Easter hare, our Easter bunny precedes the Christian tradition. The Moon-hare was the totem animal of the Moon Goddess in both Eastern and Western tradition and, together with the cat, was the familiar of many witches. The hare was the image seen on the face on the moon and many tales tell of Rhiannon the Celtic Goddess of fertility who, able to transmute into animal form at will, often chose to turn into a hare. The Moon-hare was the image carried aloft on the banner of the great warrior Queen of the Celts, Boadicea[13].

Easter is named after the Saxon Goddess of Spring - Eostre - and was a time to celebrate rebirth and the new year long before the Christian tradition celebrated the resurrection of Christ. As a celebration of spring after the death of winter, Easter and the spring equinox was always a time to celebrate fertility and new life. The most well known symbol of fertility and the most celebrated symbol of Easter is the egg, collected and painted for centuries in the rites of spring. Often they were painted red, the colour of life. Now they are made in chocolate, wrapped up in coloured foils, filled with sweets and packaged in boxes. We consume them at the rate of four per household on average during the Easter weekend[14].

Few people today recognise the symbolic significance of the chocolate consumed with the sanction of Christmas and Easter. Cocoa, the ancient Mayan's symbol of fertility and rebirth in the sacred groves and temples of Central America is now processed and packaged as a lucrative product for a mass industrialised consumer market unaware of its origins. Having lost its spiritual significance, cocoa continues to pile up fortunes for those traders and manufacturers who amass the beans whilst many of those who grow the cocoa beans never taste the processed product because they cannot afford it[15].

**Chocolate Unwrapped** The Politics of Pleasure

Once the Mayans tended their groves of trees with agricultural understanding, planetary timing and offerings to the spirits in the groves. Today, encouraged to produce huge quantities for the world market and ignorant of dangers to health, the growers of cocoa tend their crops with sprays of deadly chemicals to kill insects and unwanted plants and to artificially fertilise the ground. Mass production of cocoa is now sustained with vast quantities of pesticides, bringing in its wake waves of illness and reduced livelihood for the people who tend the cocoa, as well as damage to the environment. The life-giving plant has become a life-threatening enterprise not only in Central and South America but also in West Africa and in the South East Asia where the cocoa tree has been commercially cultivated both on smallholdings and on large plantations.

In the West today, the symbol of rebirth has become a frivolity. Chocolate appears on our television screens, promoted as a symbol of passion and romance. Its sacred and profound meaning is abandoned for advertising-led imagery with sexual associations encouraging us to consume vacuously on impulse. Dissociated from the source of our food and ignorant of the pathways to production, our 20th-century consumption of chocolate is guided by provoked demand and mediated desire.

# Passion

*Sexual Images*

Today, chocolate has a cultural significance far removed from the Mayan images of sanctity and spiritual rite. Now we readily acknowledge the reputation of chocolate as a romantic food, associated with both sex and love. This symbolism is encouraged by advertising and is promoted throughout Western popular culture. Articles on chocolate consistently draw on themes of passion, sensuality and indulgence[1] and radio chat show hosts have even used chocolate as a device to encourage the participants to reveal sexual fantasies and tales of passionate encounter[2]. Appearing regularly on television since the first night of advertising on British television in 1955, chocolate is bound together in our cultural consciousness with sentiments of sensual indulgence and images of sexual allure.

Like many foods, chocolate has symbolic significance that extends far beyond its nutritional value. Bread, known throughout centuries as the staff of life, has meant much more to the faithful consuming it at the Eucharist than its value as a complex carbohydrate. Similarly, wine symbolising the blood of Christ becomes more than an alcoholic tipple at the altar. In France, wine is the ubiquitous social lubricant signifying community and cultural identity. Milk too carries images beyond its array of nutrients, offering a sense of nurture and comfort long after we are weaned off the breast. Meat as well as milk is perceived as more than a good source of protein. Examining links between hunting, male aggression and power (and the primary focus of the British 'proper meal'), feminist thinkers argue that the consumption of meat is

18

a foundation and mode of perpetuation of patriarchal culture demonstrating men's ability to exercise control over women and food[3].

Chocolate is viewed in the developed world as a luxury. It is bought as gifts, given as presents and consumed on holidays and at festive occasions. It is boxed in fancy foils and packaged to look attractive. It is not an essential element of the diet and as such it is a treat. Yet it is affordable on a frequent and regular basis. In 1990 the British, the third biggest consumers in the world (see Table 3) spent on average £1.25 on chocolate each week[4] and on average each person in Britain consumes 8 kg of chocolate a year (see Table 2). It is available anywhere from the finest stores to the nearest garage.

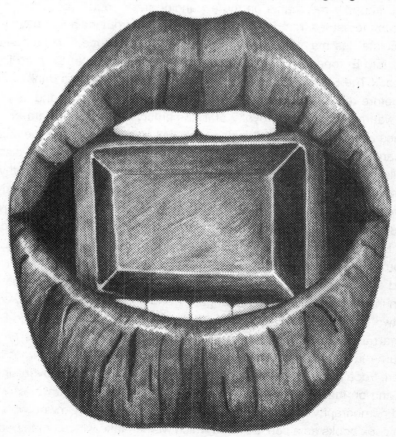

Moreover, chocolate has in the past assumed a provocative symbolic significance that has been attached to a wide variety of foods - that of the aphrodisiac. Aphrodisiac worth has been given to vegetables, fruits, nuts, seafood, fish and meat in various cultures throughout the ages. Lettuce, an aphrodisiac sacred to the fertility god Min in ancient Egypt, was considered the food to dampen desire in ancient Rome (it was into a bed of lettuce that Venus is reputed to have thrown herself to calm her grief when Adonis died). Carrots were considered by the Greeks to attract love; potatoes, first introduced into Europe from the New World, and valued at £250 per lb, were considered an aphrodisiac by virtue of their exotic origins. Many foods, newly introduced into Europe by merchants on the expanding trade routes, acquired this status, from tomatoes from South America to spices from India and beyond.

Chocolate has maintained its amorous image in European culture since its entry into Europe with the Spanish. The missionary writer Bernard Diaz, in his book *The Conquest of New Spain*[5] described Montezuma drinking chocolatl before retiring to bed with his wives and this description and its implication was not lost on the royalty of 17th-century Spain. Chocolate arrived in France accompanying the Spanish bride of Louis XIV and was the choice of the famous French courtesan, Madame du Barry, who mixed chocolate with vanilla and ambergris to drink with her lovers. In England, the wealthy celebrated chocolate as a drink to inspire passion and cocoa was included as an aphrodisiac in the 1863 edition of Culpepper's *Complete Herbal*[6]. However, whilst many of the old aphrodisiacs have succumbed to a cultural demise and become standard, nutritionally useful food (like potatoes), chocolate's amorous association has been sustained.

Food and sex are fundamental aspects of life imbued with tremendous and often intertwined meaning. Our language and popular culture readily confuse the two. Honey, for example, an aphrodisiac of the Moors, was used liberally in marriage ceremonies which often turned into sexual orgies and thus became inextricably linked with love, resulting in the modern word honeymoon. Food and sex are interwoven in films, magazines and advertising. And drawing on the feminist debate surrounding the sexual portrayal of women, food pornography has been explored by author Rosalind Coward who examines cook books as a sensual read which women take with them to bed[7].

Eating can be a highly erotic act in itself. One of the most celebrated popular portrayals of erotic eating is the contemporary Cadbury Flake advertisement. From poppy fields to hotel rooms, and now in the bath, women have been unwrapping and eating Flakes in an increasingly sensual and sexually evocative manner. Now into its fourth decade, it is one of the longest running advertising campaigns and, with sales shooting up after each new release, it is clearly one of the most successful. Eighty-four million Flake bars are now consumed each year, two out of three eaten by women[8]. After a survey to evaluate the image of the 1990s, the most recent campaign was launched in February 1991 at a cost of over £2 million. As a dark-haired woman eating a Flake in an overflowing bath replaced the image of a blond woman wearing white silk lingerie in a hotel room, the producers stressed that the new brief was to not make a sexy advertisement. However, whilst the stereotyped two dimensional image of sexual woman has been replaced by sensual woman, the Flake advertisement continues to provoke a steady trickle of complaints to the Independent Television Commission each year[9], and perpetuates the link between chocolate and sex in the minds of most of the British television viewing public.

The symbolic appeal of food is highly motivating in choosing what to eat, according to French philosopher Roland Barthes[10]. Food sociologist Paul Atkinson further suggests that we are seeking the symbolic quality rather than the nutrients when we ingest symbol-laden food[11]. Sensual expression and the desire to own one's sensuality may be an element of the motivation for many women to eat chocolate in our culture where women are struggling to reclaim their sensuality after several centuries of the subordination of feeling and emotion tempered with misogyny and moral stricture. It seems passion and pleasure are readily obtainable in material form in bite-size pieces. However, few women who eat chocolate experience it as the liberating sensual experience portrayed in the advertisements[12]. It is more likely that women experience chocolate as nurture, comfort or edible relief from premenstrual tension.

If the sexual connotation is not explicit, sexual attraction is implied in the context of romantic gifts of boxed chocolates. Whilst women buy more chocolate bars than men, men buy more chocolate boxes and it would appear they generally buy them for women. Chocolates, along with red roses, have become one of our most conventional romantic offerings. It was first carried in a box and presented to a lover, as it entered France with Princess Marie Theresa of Spain and romance has been linked to chocolate ever since. Richard Cadbury decorated his first box in 1868 with red velvet and hand painted pictures of flowers, landscapes and pretty girls. This set a precedent for a century of chocolate box imagery with the contemporary extreme represented by a European chocolate manufacturer, Lindt, who have put heart-shaped chocolates wrapped in pink foil into a box called 'Romance'.

The image of chocolate is often inseparable from its packaging. The implication of luxury and quality presented by the extravagent wrapping and package design has little to do with the product itself. The best quality chocolate bought by weight over the counter is usually minimally wrapped. Mass produced products, however, are inevitably encased in several layers of plastic, paper or foil, often all three. Boxed chocolates rest in individual paper cups or moulded casings of PVC with some pieces even then wrapped in coloured foil to enhance the image of variety and luxury when the box is opened. Increasing the number of layers around a product does not necessarily increase shelf life or prevent contamination. The various brands, in fierce competition with each other, are packaged to make them sell[13]. This 'gift' wrapping results in enormous profit margins for the manufacturer. *Marketing* magazine argues that the success of Ferrero Rocher's launch into the UK has been its packaging, which despite criticism from environmentalists, has now pushed their brands to take 2% of the UK market[14]. The cost of this excess packaging - up to 15% of the cost of the product, is passed directly on to the consumer.

The reality of packaging is that it wastes tremendous amounts of natural resources: paper made from sterile tree plantations or old growth forests; aluminium derived from bauxite, often mined and processed in tropical rainforest areas; plastics refined from oil. These processes require vast amounts of energy from finite resources and are often polluting in their manufacture. The nature of chocolate wrapping makes it almost impossible to reuse or recycle. Therefore consumers also pay for the cost of disposing of the waste created.

Springtime, from Valentine's Day to Easter, is when the British buy around one-fifth of their boxes of chocolates. Half of all boxed chocolates are bought just before Christmas and account for about half of the Christmas chocolate eating marathon, worth in total around £450 million[15]. In Japan, however, Valentine's Day is the time of greatest chocolate consumption in the year. Over 12% of all chocolate sales are made in the first two weeks of February[16] and one Tokyo department store makes a huge white chocolate sculpture of Venus de Milo for the event. Judging by sales of all kinds of chocolate worldwide, romance and passion are fitting at all times of the year. Thirty-three million Hershey Kisses are produced each day, one of the biggest sellers in the US. The latest luxury chocolate to enter Britain from Europe, which has been responsible for introducing the Italians to the commercial possibilities of both Valentine's Day and Mother's Day, is Ferrero's Baci - 'kisses' in Italian.

## Chemicals and the Body

Scientists have been looking for a substantiated chemical basis to explain the pleasure that we derive from eating chocolate. Chocolate became popular around the time that scientific thought was shaping the Western world view in the 1700s, and in the late 17th century, a Dr Stubbe published *The Indian Nectar or a Discourse Concerning Cocoa'* with references to its 'secret virtue'. Scientists have been interested in the effect of chocolate and its constituents upon our bodies ever since. In considering its sensual properties, the manufacturers refer to the 'mouth-feel' of the chocolate. Chocolate melts just below body temperature at 35° and this creates a pleasurable cooling experience as it melts in the mouth. This is what is often upheld as its sensual attraction. Scientific experimentation has investigated the possibility that chocolate contains pharmacologically active ingredients with pleasure-inducing qualities. Chocolate contains a large variety of active chemicals from amines to alkaloids. It certainly wakes you up. Chocolate contains caffeine and a milder chemical relative called theobromine, both of which are stimulants of the central nervous system and cause excitement and exhilaration if they are taken in large enough doses. Theobromine is abundant in chocolate, making up to 2% of the cocoa bean, and around 200 mg is present in a bar but its mild effects on the nervous system probably go unnoticed. It has more effect on the kidneys as a diuretic. Caffeine's most established mode of entry into our bodies is in coffee. A cup of instant coffee will contain about 65 mg of caffeine and a brewed cup contains about 115 mg. A bar of chocolate contains around 25 mg of caffeine, which is probably enough to experience a high but doesn't cause the jitters. Chocolate also contains plenty of sugar which causes an immediate physical buzz and releases a surge of energy. Added sugar constitutes half the substance of chocolate by weight. As such, chocolate, imbued with sweetness like honey before it, is fitting as a romantic food. But sugar is not a psychoactive drug. It is physiologically addictive. Whilst it may keep us coming back to chocolate to ease our sugar cravings, it is also present in the majority of foods on supermarket shelves.

The favourite pharmacological postulate for pleasure, reiterated time and again, is the molecule called phenylethylamine. This chemical is a mood elevator related to amphetamine and is found naturally in the brain. This substance is one of a group of chemicals called endorphins which play a role in facilitating feelings of happiness and euphoria and are released into the blood when we feel good. It is the runner's 'high' and the opium 'hit' and it is found in elevated concentrations in the brain when we experience love. Other chemicals such as histamine and tryptophan have also been postulated as the hedonistic candidates and they have similar roles within the central nervous system. However, all of these chemicals are found in higher concentrations in other foods which are less appealing than chocolate[17]. This doesn't undermine the endorphin's efficacy, but it shakes the often repeated theory that chocolate contains a unique love drug. To date, endorphins and pharmacological science alone don't explain our incessant attraction to chocolate.

*Advertising Myths*
Chocolate advertising has much to do with our perennial fascination and obsession with this food. Advertising campaigns turn a bar of chocolate into a brand - and with a brand, one is selling a myth. Yorkie, the Rowntree

chocolate bar, was launched with a commercial called 'Coast to Coast' which resulted in Yorkie reaching fourth place in the British confectionery market and the actor becoming a pin-up voted higher than Robert Redford in a newspaper poll[18]. The manufacturers state that advertising is arguably as important as any of the physical ingredients[19]. Aware that 70% of chocolate purchases are made on impulse, the confectionery industry is one of the biggest advertising spenders in the market today. The manufacturers spent a total of £92 million on advertising in the UK in 1990[20] (see Table 3) where Mars, spending £47 million to promote 12 brands, was the third largest corporate spender after Unilever and Procter and Gamble[21]. Nestlé spent £4 million on Kit Kat alone in the same year to keep it the best selling British brand.

It is no commercial accident that women are major consumers; women are specifically targeted by manufacturers. Cadbury have described their products as "snacks, meal replacements - and the slow, savoured eat enjoyed by women"[22]. Chocolate is endowed with gender, from the chunky Yorkie to the crumbly feminine Flake and in many advertisements, is presented to women as a sensual and sexual indulgence. Men are more likely to be portrayed eating chocolate out of physical hunger. All the major manufacturers employ similar marketing strategies in their advertising campaigns and we respond to the contradictory images in buying chocolate either because it is a secret indulgent pleasure (for women), or because it is healthy and good for us (for men, women and children). Either way, the chocolate component of the product is virtually identical once you get inside the wrapper.

With little physical substantiation for our attraction to chocolate, it seems that the symbolic associations we have of the product are paramount in our desire to consume it. Promoted by advertising campaigns, the associations we make with chocolate are mediated by the manufacturers at great expense. Yet for many women, the reality of chocolate consumption is much less glamourous than portrayed.

# Pleasure

*The Chocoholic*
*"I eat it when I'm on my period."*
*"I bought it because I'm a bit depressed, really."*
*"I haven't bought any chocolate and I wouldn't tell you if I had."*
*"I don't eat much chocolate, but I have a friend who does. She is a real chocoholic; you should speak to her."*

*"The longest that I managed to keep a bar of chocolate was four hours. I had it in the fridge and for a while I had forgotten about it, but half way through my piece of work I remembered. I challenged myself to leave it alone. 'One more page and then you can eat it; one more page and you've earned a treat.' But once in my head it took over - huge images of chocolate invaded my mind and there I was, writing 'I have a bar of chocolate in the fridge and I haven't eaten it yet'."*

*"I used to eat it at college especially in the autumn term when it was damp and dismal outside. I would come out of the mid morning lecture and go down the road to the newsagent. I'd rush in, buy a bar of chocolate on the pretence of buying a newspaper and rush out again. Sometimes I'd eat it walking back along the street, even though it made me feel vulnerable. I'd feel my body hunch up as if I was trying to hide what I was doing. I would imagine expressions of disapproval on the faces of passers-by or hear their voices chiding me as I walked past: 'you shouldn't be eating*

chocolate...you're too overweight as it is...you shouldn't be eating chocolate...is that how you got fat?'. I'd screw the wrapper up and drop it in the bin
as I was swallowing the last piece, and then return to the lecture room wearing an air of defiance but with a cloying dissatisfaction lying in my stomach."

"She would buy it when she did the big weekly supermarket shop. She would
buy ten or fifteen bars at a time, not the big bars but the small size, either
wrapped up three to a bag in nylon string or off the trays by the till. She kept
it in the cupboard in the kitchen from where the kids would often grab one
after dinner to eat in front of the TV as dessert. She would slip back into the
kitchen after dinner to go and do the ironing. She would put her wrappers in
the bin under the sink."

"...flowers, perfume maybe ... no, there's nothing romantic about chocolate
whatsoever."

The chocoholic appears to us in her various guises as the compulsive eater,
the woman who indulges intermittently and the woman with a 'sweet tooth'.
She can be found in most newsagents, supermarkets and speciality shops
where the focus of her attention is cheap and is displayed in abundance.

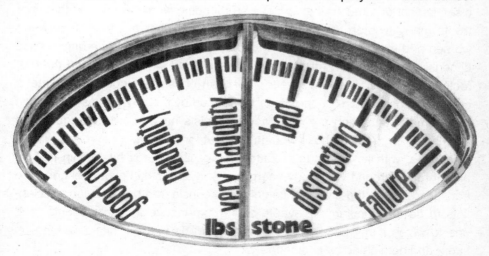

Sometimes she finds herself caught in a fraught moment of indecision, hesitating over her urge to gorge on a bar of rich, sweet chocolate but held back by inner voices recalling feelings of guilt, insecurities about her body image and her self-loathing at her faltering strength of will. Abstaining from chocolate may be a challenging experience to put herself through. Nevertheless many women test themselves this way, perhaps regularly, as the will-power to diet falters and chocolate seems like a welcome reprieve, a deserved reward for those aeons of abstinence and self-control. If she is not eating out of hunger and a need for comfort, perhaps she is eating out of anger and a desire to swallow her feelings, or simply because she is about to start her period and is wallowing through waves of emotion. She may simply enjoy her chocolate as a guilt-free treat or a taste of luxury, eating for energy and pleasure, yet few women escape obsessions with food. Cycles of consternation over body image can be played out endlessly as fashion dictates forms of beauty and we feel tremendous pressures to conform and be accepted by our society.

As chocolate has acquired the mythical reputation as a food with the power to inspire passion and banish loneliness, and still be readily available to all, it is women who respond overwhelmingly to this message. Chocolate addiction has acquired a frivolous profile in the media, yet it is only one highly publicised aspect of a much deeper issue surrounding women and food that confronts many women in Western society today[1]. The relationship between women and the food they eat extends beyond physical and pharmacological dimensions, as women often resort to using food when they need nurture, feeling and satisfaction on levels other than physical hunger. Chocolate is certainly considered to be the major binge food by therapy groups for women with compulsive eating problems and therapists have noted[2] is frequently a first choice for many of those women who eat for comfort.

Chocolate, with its high sugar content, gives an energy hit. Within half an hour it races around your body energising you and making you feel good. To eat sugar and fat together is a combination considered by behavioural scientists to be a particularly enjoyable eating experience for most people[3] and one to which many people have become addicted as our diet is laden with sugar and dominated by fatty food.

Those working in this field, such as Susie Orbach[4], have recognised that, for many women to come to terms with eating compulsively, they must explore underlying emotional needs and their individual personal relationship with food. In a safe space where women come together for support and emotional understanding, women have been able to unlock the key that keeps them returning to chocolate or bread or biscuits in sudden irresistible compulsive urges. Within the safety of a supportive group, women are recognising that they turn to thick, sweet, heavy food instead of feeling an array of emotions that arise and are seen as difficult and so are swallowed away. They recognise that they do not have a physical hunger and what they want is not food but a hug, a run around the park or to express their anger. Women will eat food such as chocolate when they are longing for comfort, when they need emotional nourishment, when they are stuffing down feelings of pain, loneliness, anger, frustration. It takes courage to express our feelings to others and inner resolve to experience difficult emotions in ourselves.

Women may experience chocolate as a soothing and nurturing experience, an association which may be learnt when we were young. Mothers probably gave us chocolate as a treat and grandmothers gave us chocolate with love, but we were also fed chocolate to keep us occupied, quiet and out of the way. How often were we encouraged to eat a bar of chocolate when what we wanted to do was to scream or shout or cry and so we chocolate-coated our hurt feelings? In doing so, we were set a precedent at an early age to swallow our feelings because it was easier not to show them.

### Dieting, Binging and Battles

The connection between fat, food and feelings is not conscious for many women. Often the woman who feels she is fat will be caught up in chaotic eating in cycles of dieting, binging and battles of self-will over food. Food is a battle ground in which items such as chocolate become arch-enemies. Yet fat is not, as slimming sheets and diet clinics inform us, about lack of self-control or will power; it is about sexuality, comfort, emotion, protection and fear.

Our relationship with food is also influenced by our personal perceptions of body image and cultural depiction of beauty, as Naomi Wolf so conclusively portrayed in *The Beauty Myth*[5]. Many women who think they are fat are not. Many women who think they are fat would not have done so 20 years ago and most women who think they are fat are not happy with it. You don't have to be fat, however, to want to change your body. A 1984 survey of 33,000 women conducted in the American magazine *Glamour* showed 75% believed they were fat whereas only 25% were medically overweight and 45% of women who were actually underweight thought they were too fat[6]. Many women today do not like their bodies and have inflicted all kinds of torture on themselves from dieting to surgery to help make it right.

Eating disorders are more common among women[7]. According to the popular women's press over half of all women suffer from some form of disordered eating. Women are internalising their discontent and are taking their suffering out on themselves, damaging themselves rather than others. Compulsive eating has a long history[8] which, together with obesity, is now dramatically on the increase[9]. The incidence of anorexia is spiralling; one survey identified 1% of British adolescent girls as anorexic[10]. Bulimia was first used to describe the cycle of binging and purging in the mid-1970s and is now a household word. This illness, together with anorexia, now afflicts 1 in every 100 women in Western Europe[11] and is increasing by 6000 individuals each year in the UK[12]. Ninety-five per cent of these cases are women. Eating disorders start young. One study found one in four girls as young as nine to be worried about their body shape and to be dieting before they enter their teens[13].

Women throughout the Western world are waging war on their bodies with food. According to reports up to 90% of all women have used some form of weight control to get thinner[14]. The slimming business has grown to multi-million pound industry on the back of this insecurity, concern and self-loathing.

Women throughout the rich North are choosing to starve themselves in the face of plenty, as the women of the South struggle to provide a diet of adequate nutritional value from limited resources. For the individual on a diet, food is a complete obsession occupying most wakeful moments with calorie counting and a manic depressive oscillation between feeling good when you have refrained from food and guilty when you have eaten. Binging is what you do when you can't keep this starvation regime going and it is not surprising that chocolate is a primary binge food, as it is composed substantially of fat and sugar and it has the potential to be a fattening food thereby eliciting a great amount of guilt.

*Beauty and Guilt*

Promoted by women who are manifestly thinner than the average woman consuming it, the portrayal of body image is especially pertinent to chocolate advertising. Feminists have been challenging the presentation of beauty and body image for many years and the depiction of women in the media currently incites around 9% of the annual 2500 complaints to the Independent Television Commission[15]. Whilst chocolate is a product which holds associations of sensuality and romance, it is also recognised as a food which makes you fat. In a culture where thinness is upheld as the paragon of beauty in women, the consumption of fattening food is an act which often elicits guilt and anxiety. Indeed, whilst we become absorbed in the advertising myth, chocolate, considered the principal binge food of many women, is in reality consumed with much less glamour than that portrayed.

Marilyn Monroe would be considered relatively fat if she graced our magazine covers today. The reality is that, over the last decade, the weight of top models has dropped from 8% less than the average woman to 23% below that of the average woman[16]. The size of women portrayed in pornographic magazines has become thinner whilst the size of the average woman has in fact become bigger, resulting in increased clothes' sizes over the last decade. Whilst enlightened articles about food and eating appear in some women's magazines today, they are surrounded on all sides by advertisements for cosmetics, clothes, perfumes and body products, draped over culturally esteemed images of mannequin-thin women. In receiving the overriding message that to be thin is to be beautiful and that to be beautiful is to be valued, is encouraging increasing numbers of women to be unhappy in their bodies, to starve themselves and to feel guilty about eating.

To uphold images of female beauty that are unobtainable for the majority, to value those women who have met the criteria of beauty and ignore and undermine those who fail to meet the generic standard is to disempower the majority of women who spend much of their waking lives and their hard-earned income working to obtain this externally imposed and gratuitously bestowed cultural value. Moreover, it is exhausting for those who achieve it at the expense of all the other avenues of self expression and creative achievement.

How ironic that so many chocolate advertisements continue to convey images of beauty when they are trying to sell the very thing that is forbidden, banned, dangerous and to be avoided at all costs if one is to be and remain beautiful. What outrageous satire that the women who advertise chocolate on television become icons of contemporary beauty, when the product they sell is feared by any woman who has dieted in the name of body image. What contradiction that the models who sell us our guilt-making chocolate binges are the thin, perfect personifications of 1990s good looks. What phenomenal marketing success, that the product they sell is turned to by women in their droves, not because chocolate makes women beautiful and thereby valued and admired, but because it makes them feel better about the very fact that they are not.

# Goodness

*A Healthy Food?*

The basic ingredients of chocolate can be found on any chocolate bar wrapper: cocoa solids, cocoa fat, refined sugar, milk, vegetable fats, emulsifier, flavourings. Drawing on primary ingredients and basic manufacturing techniques developed in the 19th century[1], today scientific research and technological innovation has resulted in a sophisticated product from an increasingly automated chocolate factory. Throughout, the manufacturers have promulgated the message that chocolate is a food filled with goodness[2].

Contemporary chocolate manufacture is a highly technological process not just in view of the machinery used in production but also in the ingredients themselves, as the manufacturers seek to adjust and modify the product, which today bears very little resemblance to the Mayan concoction or the courtesan love potion, either in constitution or execution.

The manufacturing process begins with the release of the cocoa from the cocoa beans. The brown shell of the beans is cracked into pieces using rollers and discarded, leaving the inner 'nib' which consists of 50% cocoa butter and 50% non-fat cocoa solids. The fat is colourless and the solids brown and both contain the all-important cocoa flavour.

The nib is then roasted to bring out the cocoa flavour and this stage may also be accompanied by the first of several chemical processes, using alkaline chemicals such as potassium carbonate, or sodium hydroxide, to improve the flavour and colour. After cooling, the cocoa nib is ground to produce a thick chocolate liquid known as liquor, which is then passed through the

powerful hydraulic press to extract the cocoa butter. Residual fat may be extracted using a chemical such as a highly refined petroleum solvent. After extraction, cocoa butter is subject to further chemical processes including cleaning, bleaching, and deodorising using superheated steam (to weaken the flavour for milk chocolate). The remains of the pressed liquor, a solid block of cocoa known as the cake, will become cocoa powder or drinking chocolate after more grinding, alkalising, flavouring and sifting.

Whilst many of the manufacturers buy beans to produce chocolate from raw ingredients, these initial stages of chocolate manufacture are increasingly performed by specialized 'processing' companies who sell the cocoa cake and cocoa butter on to manufacturers. Plain chocolate is produced by mixing the ingredients without milk. In the manufacture of milk chocolate, cocoa butter is mixed with liquor, milk, sugar, other vegetable fats and emulsifier. Milk chocolate became more popular than plain at the end of the last century with the development of a milk drying process. The milk used today is usually in the form of milk crumb which is produced by dissolving refined sugar in milk and then evaporating the water to produce condensed milk. Chocolate liquor is then mixed with the sweetened condensed milk and the mixture is dried. To produce milk chocolate, the chocolate crumb is mixed with cocoa butter and sometimes extra liquor or sugar and the mixture is ground through a series of steel rollers until the cocoa particles are refined to such a degree that they cannot be felt in the mouth.

A crucial process known as conching takes place after refining, whereby the ground flakes of chocolate are mixed into a smooth chocolate liquid. This stirring, which can last for several days, takes place in large vats known as 'conches' (from the Latin for 'shell', due to their shape), and is designed to improve the texture and flavour of the final product. It is the conching process which has been the focus of technological research in the chocolate manufacturing process in recent years. A comparatively slow process and therefore costly in terms of time and energy, recent research efforts have focused on reducing this time by pre-treatment of the cocoa mass[3].

Conching is followed by another advanced technological process known as tempering. The liquid chocolate is mixed and cooled under carefully controlled conditions to ensure that the fat sets in its most stable form. The role of the fat is to coat the particles of sugar, cocoa and milk so that they combine to form a solid bar. Tempering is an important influence on the final texture, appearance and shelf-life of the product.

In addition to cocoa butter, other vegetable fats, emulsifiers and butter fat are also used to combine the ingredients into a stable form and to produce the distinctive texture and 'mouth-feel'. Lecithin, the substance most commonly used as an emulsifier in chocolate, occurs naturally and is commercially obtained from soybeans, ground cotton seed, sunflower oil and rape seed oil. Lecithin is extracted by leaching with a solvent and may also be bleached using hydrogen peroxide and benzoyl peroxide. In addition, a small quantity of dairy butter is used to prevent 'bloom', the mottled appearance which indicates that fat or sugar is beginning to separate out of the chocolate.

During tempering, or just after, ingredients such as fruit and nuts, and flavourings such as vanilla, cinnamon and lemon oil can be added to the liquid chocolate. It is then poured into chocolate bar moulds and passes through cooling chambers until it sets and the moulded bars are turned out ready for wrapping. For boxed chocolates, soft fillings are poured into a moulded chocolate shell and finished off with a layer of chocolate; whilst hard fillings are passed on a continuous belt beneath a curtain of liquid chocolate. Wrapping and boxing are largely automated, facilitating the incredible speeds of production which the factories are now capable of. Wispa bars roll off the conveyor belts at speeds of over 1,600 every minute, replete with computer calibrated air bubbles. In the face of such a technological feat of food production, only quality control is left receiving a human touch.

*Additives*

Whilst food technologists are initiating complex developments in the chocolate making process, and are producing an increasingly sophisticated processed product, manufacturers are circumscribed by British labelling regulations[4], which specify what can and cannot be called 'chocolate'. Chocolate must contain not less than 35% total dry cocoa solids of which at least 14% must be dry non-fat cocoa solids and at least 18% cocoa butter. Legal requirements for plain and milk chocolate specify varying proportions (plain chocolate must contain at least 30% cocoa solids, and milk chocolate either 23% cocoa solids and 14% milk or 20% cocoa solids and 20% milk). Up to 5% vegetable fat may be added.

One of the most important areas at the moment for research and development into chocolate ingredients is in the field of added vegetable fats called Cocoa Butter Equivalents (CBEs) and Cocoa Butter Improvers (CBIs). Currently, of all the major producer countries, only the UK, Ireland and Denmark permit the use of CBEs and CBIs, up to a level of 5% in products labelled 'chocolate'. CBEs and CBIs are vegetable fats which can replace cocoa butter in chocolate recipes which, whilst having similar chemical properties at a much lower cost, can also be used to influence texture and other qualities. They are usually made from palm-oil mixed with other vegetable fats in a blend which can be varied to provide different properties[5]. The use of other fats is an important factor in the profit margins of the chocolate industry, since cocoa butter is the most expensive chocolate ingredient. Originally developed during the 1970s when the price of cocoa rose on the world market, the difference in cost between cocoa butter and, for example, palm oil, is substantial and underlies the pressure from manufacturers to be allowed to modify the product and the legislation.

In most other EC countries, CBEs are not permitted. But the European trade association CAOBISCO, have campaigned for CBIs to be permitted in 'chocolate' products EC-wide, arguing that vegetable fats should be permitted to the 5% level in all member countries from 1993. Chocolate recipes using CBIs can also give a longer shelf-life in hot climates than pure cocoa-butter products which has potentially rewarding implications for the chocolate manufacturers whose sights are set on selling to the rest of the world, now that consumer markets in the North are close to saturation. In the US, the development of 'tropical chocolate' is well advanced, using a variety of high-melting fats which prevent it from melting in the heat and the Japanese have patented similar processes. However, this chocolate tends to have a 'waxy' texture requiring the addition of further fats — sorbitan stearates — to modify the impact of the cocoa butter replacements. The use of these additives is likely to be an increasing feature of chocolate ingredient technology in the future[6].

While manufacturers' chocolate recipes are trade secrets, every bar of chocolate contains flavourings which are referred to but not always detailed on the wrapper. Several thousand artificial, natural and naturally-derived flavourings are used today by the food industry, which remain largely uncontrolled by the British Government and the EC. British food regulations specify that any flavouring may be added to chocolate provided it is not chocolate flavour. Flavourings need only be named if they provide a predominant flavour or odour (for example, a peppermint filling), in which case the label must indicate whether the flavour is derived from its natural source ('coffee flavoured'), or is artificial ('coffee taste' or 'coffee flavour')[7].

Also permitted in chocolate confectionery are a variety of colours, antioxidants, emulsifiers, sweeteners and other additives with a variety of purposes. Mars, for example, use all of the following in some of their products: citric acid, sodium citrate, gum arabic, glycerol, pectin, glycerol monostearate, sorbitan stearate, sodium tristearate, sodium bicarbonate, and carnauba wax. They also use the following colours: quinoline yellow, carmoisine, sunset yellow, patent blue V, brilliant green S, titanium dioxide, ponceau, indigo carmine, B-carotene. Flavourings, however, apart from ethyl vanillin, a vanilla flavouring which is found in most chocolate products, often remain nameless. The debate surrounding food additives has raged now for over a decade, between those who believe our health is at risk from the quantities of additional chemicals added to our food and the food industry and their supporters who argue that additives are essential to food production and who defend their position of making processed food more attractive and palatable and therefore more profitable[8]. Public opinion turned against food additives during the early 1980s when the UK succumbed to an EC directive in 1983 which required the labelling of additives on food. Shortly thereafter, *E is for Additives*[9] became a best seller, promoting discussion about carcinogenicity and long term health effects of eating additives and the connection between them and hyperactivity in children. Food producers and retailers recognising the strength of public concern responded by reducing the number of chemicals used in the manufacturing process - yet today there are still over 3000 added chemicals in our diet and increasing concern about the types and quantities of additives in food and drink consumed especially by young children[10].

*Health Effects*
Some additives cause allergic skin reactions or asthma in some people; others are known to be carcinogenic in animal tests. Of the colourings and flavourings used in confectionery, a number are now generally considered a health risk. Quinoline Yellow, a food colouring, for example is one of the azo dyes derived from coal tar, which are banned from use in baby foods because they are dangerous to asthmatics, hyperactive children, migraine and eczema sufferers[11]. In the UK, the Hyperactive Children's Support Group, founded by Mrs Sally Bunday, has campaigned to alert parents and politicians to the dangers of additive-laden diets in children. The group promotes the Feingold Diet, which involves the elimination from the diet of all foods and additives which appear to affect the child's behaviour or cause a medical problem. The results of studies, together with the group's own data base, have produced a list of food items to be avoided by hyperactive and food-intolerant children. Chocolate is amongst the top five 'problem' foods, whilst azo dyes like tartrazine and quinoline yellow, are known to be particularly likely to cause reactions. Research has not yet established the reasons for such effects, but after widespread resistance, the medical establishment is beginning to accept the results of such trials. In the meantime, whilst the Ministry of Agriculture, Fisheries and Food is sufficiently convinced by the available evidence to have banned the dyes from all food specially prepared

for babies, azo dyes are still to be found in most brightly coloured confectionery[12].

Other chemicals readily added to our food are also less than wholesome - ethyl vanillin is an artificial vanilla flavouring used in virtually all chocolate, which is made from lignin, a waste product of the paper industry, produced by treating wood chips with sulphur-based chemicals or alcohol. In testing, it has been shown to be a skin irritant that produces a burning sensation and eczema, and may cause pigmentation of the skin[13]. Many additives have yet to be thoroughly examined for health effects, and the effects of consuming cocktails of chemicals as we do when eating any single food product remains untested and unknown. Yet chemicals continue to be sprinkled liberally throughout our food whilst scientific and industrial intransigence prevails. The difference in current legislation between nations, demonstrates the disparate views on the inclusion of these chemicals in our food. In general, British controls on additives are currently weaker than many other industrialised countries[14], yet with the finalisation of the EC trade standards, the UK approved list of around 300 chemicals is set to swell to 400 as European trade harmonisation assumes a low common denominator rather than a higher standard, taking the progression towards an uncontaminated diet on a retrograde path[15].

*Fat and Sugar in our Diet*
Whilst concern associated with the use of additives is important in maintaining safe food, a broad consensus of medical opinion is now re-evaluating the health effects from the balance of the primary components of our diet. Fat and sugar have been fundamental to the Western diet since the time of the Second World War when the prevailing ideology was to provide food to make people big and strong. Such advice however failed to investigate the ensuing effects on the body in the form of the chronic diseases now associated with Western diet and Western culture.

Milk chocolate is permitted to contain up to 55% sucrose. Many chocolate bars with sugary fillings will contain a good deal more. Over half of every mouthful of chocolate is therefore refined sugar. The UK has one of the highest levels of sugar consumption in the world, averaging around 100 lb a year per person (almost 2 lb a week)[16]. This means around a quarter of our calorie intake now comes from processed sugars, around 7% of which comes from chocolate and confectionery[17]. In our culture, our addiction to sugar begins early. For children of pre-school age, sugar contributes between 25 and 29% of their total daily energy intake[18], and in a recent survey of Northumberland schoolchildren, the main sources of sugar in their diet, in order of importance, were: confectionery, table sugar, soft drinks and fruit juices, biscuits and cakes, and sweet puddings[19].

The link between refined sugars and tooth decay is now so widely accepted that the Health Education Authority (HEA) stated in 1990 that 'Extensive evidence suggests that sugars are the most important factor in the causation of dental cavities'[20]. In 1983, 48% of British 5 year olds had some tooth decay and, by the age of 12, an average of 4.3% teeth were affected. By the age of 15, nearly all children had some tooth decay. The evidence on links between sugar and tooth decay has particular relevance to the chocolate industry. The weight of research now shows that refined sugars are far more damaging than intrinsic sugars (fructose found in fruit and lactose found in milk), and that the frequency of consumption is the most important factor in the development of tooth decay[21]. Tooth decay is caused by acid, produced by bacteria in a film of sugars and proteins known as plaque. The bacteria interacts with sugar to form an acid which attacks tooth enamel. Enamel which has begun to soften because of acid attack can regenerate itself, provided it is free of acid for a reasonable period of time, but a frequent sugar intake will prevent this regeneration. The 1990 Handbook of Dental Health for Health Visitors states that "The most important message which must be conveyed to mothers is that consumption of sugar-containing food and drinks should be limited as far as possible to mealtimes."[22] A consideration not included in the message of the Milky Way slogan "The Sweet You Can Eat Between Meals Without Ruining Your Appetite".

Sugar is also linked to numerous other chronic health conditions including obesity, diabetes, heart disease, hypertension and gallstones, although the physiological mechanisms have yet to be established[23]. Out of 100 reports on diet published between 1961 and 1991, analysed in a comprehensive survey by Geoffrey Cannon (chair of the National Food Alliance), 82 recommend that the amount of added sugar (refined from sugar cane or beet) that we consume in our diet be reduced[24]. This includes the World Health Organisation and the latest and long-awaited report published in 1991 by COMA (the Department of Health's Committee on Medical Aspects of Food Policy)[25], who recommended a decrease in sugar consumption to 10% of total energy intake. For the average individual, this would mean a drop in consumption by around 50%. The report declares that refined sugar is completely unnecessary in our diet, since it provides only empty calories and no nutrients at all.

Of course such views have not been allowed to inform public opinion without some retaliatory action from those most at risk from a scientific and medical consensus favouring a healthier diet by a lower sugar consumption — the sugar industry — whose largest UK customer is Cadbury Schweppes[26]. The Sugar Bureau launched its notorious 'hummingbird' advert as part of a three-year £12 million advertising campaign in 1990, heralding sugar as a natural food, in respect of which the Independent Television Commission - the TV advertising regulatory body - was swamped by complaints about its misleading nature[27]. More recently, the Health Education Authority was the target of the public relations arm of the food industry — the Food and Drink Federation — which challenged the accuracy of the promotional material at a HEA-sponsored conference on ways to reduce sugar in our diet[28].

Milk chocolate must also, by legislative definition, contain a minimum of 25% fat. With the addition of fillings, most chocolate lines will contain considerably more. Yet fats, especially hard, saturated fats, like cocoa butter, are the target of health promoters the world over.

About 70% of deaths in the UK are caused by heart disease, cancer and strokes which are thought to be due to some extent to our diet and are therefore avoidable. Obesity is a cause for health concern throughout the Western World with one in three people in the UK considered overweight. In 1984, according to WHO figures, Britain had the highest rates of premature death from heart disease in the developed world[29]. "Overall, diet related diseases kill more Britons each year than smoking, drugs, accidents and AIDS put together, so some kind of action is desperately needed."[30]

Although the causes are complex and far from fully understood, fats, especially saturated fats, are implicated in a number of the 'preventable diseases', especially heart disease, obesity, high blood pressure, and some common cancers[31]. Reports examining our diet overwhelmingly recommend a reduction in fat intake, especially of saturated fats. The COMA report stated that 42.6% of the British calorie intake is provided by fats and called for a reduction to 35%, of which only 15% should be derived from saturated fats[32]. With 93 out of the 100 reports in Geoffrey Cannon's survey suggesting that a reduction in fat consumption was beneficial to health, medical consensus has clearly become established[33].

In light of these re-assessments of what constitutes a healthy diet, the major ingredients of chocolate, namely sugar, milk and cocoa butter, are being increasingly condemned as the components of a diet which undermines our long-term good health. The HEA makes reference to the fact that there are no 'good' or 'bad' foods only 'good' or 'bad' diets[34] — readily endorsed by the manufacturers — nevertheless chocolate, being fat and sugar laden is the quintessential representative of an unhealthy diet.

Contemporary diets are the diets of the processed food and snacking culture which has increased to the point that now around 75% of the food we eat is processed, coming from a conveyer-belt rather than directly from the land[35]. Produced in a manner devoid of human interaction, the sustenance that we receive from our food rests solely on its ingredients. With the consensus of medical opinion demonstrating that a diet high in fat and sugar is unhealthy, the processed packaged chocolate bar, upheld as a symbol of goodness by the manufacturers since advertising began, is an exemplification of that which is increasingly unappealing as a food for good health. With most of our food processed and packaged, the quality of our food has become confused with the quality of technological application, the use of which enables manufacturers to emphasise the use of wholesome ingredients whilst sanctioning the use of chemicals to facilitate the process, reduce its costs or modify the appearance of the final product.

# Purity

*Pre-packaged Pesticides*

In January 1990, post-Christmas chocoholics awoke to a headline in the Mail on Sunday[1], alerting them to the presence of pesticide residues in chocolate. The Mail, prompted by an article on cocoa and pesticides appearing in the December issue of *The Food Magazine* [2], had commissioned residue analysis on popular bars of chocolate and results had tested positive for lindane in four out of seven brands[3]. Hitherto associated with fruit and farm crops, pesticide residues in a product as processed and packaged as chocolate, were nevertheless a predictable development, after lindane and dichlorvos residues were revealed to contaminate imported cocoa beans in 1989[4].

The levels of residues found today in chocolate are not considered harmful by either the industry or the government. However, despite campaigns for

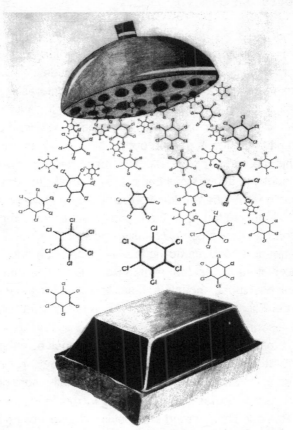

pesticide-free food and accessible information, we still live in great ignorance of the facts surrounding the traces of pesticides that we consume daily in our food. Information on pesticide residues in food generally is shrouded in obscurity, and scientific evaluation of safety is hotly contested.

### Residue Testing

Whilst we are unaware of what pesticides are used and what residues are present in the foods we eat, including the quantities of these and the consequent health effects, the government has been testing food for residues since 1966. Known as the Total Diet Study[5], this relies on the equivalent of a spot check on residues every five or so years, rather than providing a comprehensive survey of pesticide residue levels in our diet.

Categorising food into groupings statistically evaluated to represent the average diet, over a year of study a basket of food is bought fortnightly and prepared, blended and tested to reveal the extent of pesticides. However, the survey fails to examine the full range of goods in the food stores by checking only a selected number of the food categories and testing for a limited range of pesticides[6]. With the extrapolation of data from one basket-load of food to the total population, little testing is carried out relative to the amount of food we consume and this method does not allow for the varied and diverse diets eaten around the country. Such a small sample loses the variations in levels of residue on products from different locations and any highly contaminated product will be diluted in its category in the blender. Better able to determine general trends rather than give a comprehensive view of levels of residues in our food, such infrequent random sampling leaves much to be desired in presenting an accurate picture of residue levels in our diet[7]. The fruit and preserves category, which includes chocolate, tested positive for lindane in 1980 at up to 100 parts per billion (ppb)[8] but has not been tested for organochlorine residues in the test programme since.

Other specific food testing has been more comprehensive, although has failed to test chocolate in the last ten years[9]. Set up by the Ministry of Agriculture, Fisheries and Food (MAFF) in 1977, and initially more concerned with pesticide practice on the farm than poisons in the food, the Working Party on Pesticide Residues has carried out special studies looking at specific foods and certain pesticides. More recently, it has begun continuous examination of major commodities, such as bread, milk and potatoes, later adding cereals, animal products and fruit and vegetables. The Working Party's figures released in 1990 form the most complete report on residue levels published in the UK to date. These studies have revealed data showing greater cause for concern than ever shown in the Total Diet Studies. Whilst the agrochemical industry confidently stated that "the British public should have every confidence in its diet, according to the latest results of the Government's monitoring of pesticide residues in food"[10] and referred to the Government report as "reassuring"[11], pesticides were found in 32% of the samples and over 2% of the tests exceeded statutory safe levels. Indeed the chairman of the Working Party, Dr Stanley, is aware that there is "no such thing as pesticide-free food in Britain"[12]. Whilst the Government has always claimed publicly that residues in food are harmless, a report released in 1988 was less confident and talked of the "bucket and shovel" techniques used to apply post-harvest pesticides and the concealed "health hazard to man" posed by some pesticides[13].

Legal controls on the permissible levels of pesticide residues in food in the UK were set in 1988, in response to EC pressure. Prior to this, there was no enforceable limit on the amount of pesticides allowed to be present in food at all. These set levels, called maximum residue levels (MRL), apply to only 62 pesticides and these are applied only to specified primary foods such as wheat, potatoes and milk, rather than processed foods like chocolate[14]. MRL are not a measure of safety for the person eating the food, but indicate whether the farmers have used the pesticides correctly, being based upon the guidelines for good agricultural practices as well as toxicity studies.

More descriptive of the risk to health is a measure of residue called the acceptable daily intake (ADI) which is derived from toxicological evidence and of which recommended levels have been established by the United Nations. The World Health Organisation (WHO) and the Food & Agricultural Organisation (FAO) sponsor the UN Codex Committee on Pesticide Residues (Codex), the aim of which is to establish the levels of pesticide considered safe to consume. However, Codex is an unelected body accountable only to governments, and is strongly influenced by industry. Governments invite corporate representatives to participate, and both Nestle and Jacobs Suchard attended the 23rd session of the Codex Committee on Pesticide Residues (CCPR) in April 1991 on the Swiss delegation[15]. The views of consumers and environmentalists remain unrepresented, unless they are invited to join a particular delegation which happens rarely. Whilst nations may determine and implement their own safety level legislation, Codex standards are considered a bench mark and have been assumed by some governments, including the UK, where MRL do not vary from those set by Codex.

Many nations, including the US and Australia, currently implement stricter standards than Codex[16]. Yet the current round of GATT talks, in the interest of free trade, is sacrificing a higher standard of public health by seeking to implement the Codex levels as statutory residue levels on a worldwide basis.

By enforcing the adoption of a world food standard which is often the lowest common denominator, and with the prospect of being unable to enforce any condition which could be considered protectionist or confer unfair advantage, such as tighter residue standards, the movement towards free trade is set to limit the right of nations to set stricter health standards[17].

So is it only the Sunday newspapers who are checking our chocolate for pesticide residues? Despite being one of the biggest selling food sectors in the UK, confectionery was not looked at in the recent government testing programme and hasn't been included in the Total Diet Study in the last ten years. Most supermarkets monitor residue levels in some food, especially fruit and vegetables, by requesting comprehensive data from crop suppliers and produce growers. In some cases they also conduct their own tests, using both UK and additional non-statutory EC MRL as guidelines. For chocolate, however, we have to rely on the manufacturers to check themselves. According to the Biscuit, Cake, Chocolate and Confectionery Alliance (BCCCA), the main representative of the chocolate industry in the UK, the industry has been testing for pesticides since 1972. Manufacturers are not required to publish their results and generally keep this information to themselves under the guise of corporate security or commercial confidentiality. However, results were released to MAFF in 1987 and, prompted by direct questions from the London Food Commission, the industry released residue test results in 1989[18].

The BCCCA tests for 32 pesticide residues in cocoa beans including organophosphates, carbamates and organochlorines. Their results have shown residues of all three kinds of pesticides in the cocoa beans including lindane, dieldrin and DDT (all organochlorine pesticides), the use of which has been campaigned against by the Pesticide Action Network. Whilst DDT is no longer used, and aldrin and dieldrin no longer manufactured, their long persistence in the soil means residues are still detected in the beans. As a result of its widespread use, lindane is the most frequently found pesticide residue in cocoa beans. Whilst 50-60% of the residue remains in the husk surrounding the cocoa and is discarded in processing, the remainder stays in the nib, where the fat soluble organochlorine residues are retained in the cocoa butter, whilst the cocoa powder is virtually residue free[19]. According to the BCCCA in 1989, their results demonstrated the extent of lindane residues, apparent in 60% of the samples of cocoa beans[20]. Supporting the results of the Mail on Sunday's tests which found 20 ppb of lindane in chocolate products, residues of an average concentration of 25 ppb were found in cocoa beans[21]. More recent results from the BCCCA show lindane in 20% of the samples at an average of 38 ppb[22]. The industry considers that their results over the years show that organophosphates, such as dichlorvos, and carbamates like propoxur are almost completely metabolised by the plant with "only trace amounts of breakdown products found in the cocoa", and that organochlorines like lindane (which are more persistent) are found "only in very low concentrations"[23]. Whilst 5% of those samples exceeded 100 ppb lindane, none exceeded 1,000 ppb, the Codex standard MRL for lindane in cocoa[24]. According to the BCCCA, pesticide residue levels examined in their biannual testing programme consistently fall within Codex guidelines[25].

The procedure adopted by Cocoa de Zaan (the largest cocoa processor in Amsterdam) demonstrates diligent attention to a residue testing programme. The Dutch processors examine every 1.5 tonnes of the 30,000 tonnes of cocoa they process annually. They test in particular for organochlorine residues, especially lindane and DDT, and find that most of the contamination is caused by lindane. According to the laboratory manager "only" 1-2% of the cocoa beans they process have residue levels over the legal limit and, when high levels occur, in order to meet the more stringent statutory requirements of Swiss buyers, they are diluted with less contaminated stock[26].

*Body Intakes and Acceptable Doses*
As the industry noted in 1989[27], no regulations exist in the UK determining acceptable levels of residues in cocoa. Cocoa contaminated with lindane, propoxur or any of the other chemicals found in the beans is not covered by any of those 62 statutory MRL, although Codex recommend a level for lindane in cocoa of 1,000 ppb which is upheld by the EC, whilst half that concentration is the statutory limit in Switzerland. Whilst representing an industry comprising one of the biggest-selling food sectors in the UK, the BCCCA considers that "cocoa contributes so little to the UK diet and so it is not surprising that UK maximum residue levels have not been established". Thus

the industry refers to the Codex MRL for guidance, but has no obligation to meet them[28].

By current standards of safety, the concentrations of these chemical residues found in chocolate are not considered to be harmful. The industry points out that "regular testing shows that levels of residues are consistently below acceptable daily intakes (ADI)"[29]. At the levels found in cocoa, an adult eating a small chocolate bar would receive less than 1% of the Codex ADI of lindane from this source and would have to consume a ton of chocolate to exceed it[30]. Indeed, the industry is confident that "in the light of present toxicological advice they [residues] do not present a hazard to health"[31].

Determined by Codex, the acceptable daily intake of a pesticide refers to the amount of pesticide which we can consume daily in safety. It is derived from animal experiments where animals are given pesticides at different doses to determine the level of pesticide at which there is an observable effect upon them over a lifetime. This figure is divided by ten on an assumption that humans are ten times more sensitive to these chemicals than other species and then by ten again, assuming that the most sensitive person is ten times more sensitive than the average person. This figure, with its safety margin of 100 on a range of animal toxicity tests, is then considered to be the amount of pesticide which is safe for people to consume every day for a lifetime[32].

The assumptions in constructing this analysis and margin of safety, however, serve only to demonstrate our lack of knowledge about the effects of pesticide residues on the human body. Whilst such testing has proven useful as an indicator of health hazards, uncertainties circumscribe the extent of the validity of this approach. Extrapolating data from animal experiments to humans is a complacent logic, fraught with difficulties as it is not possible to be sure that animals and humans will react in the same way to any chemical. Some researchers believe, for example, that lindane is more dangerous to humans than animals[33]. Also, there is widespread and hotly contended debate over the prediction of the human carcinogenic potential of pesticides from animal tests. Indeed, concern about the limitations of animal testing prompted the House of Commons Committee on Pesticides and Health to recommend that an immediate evaluation of the use of animal testing for pesticide toxicity be carried out in 1987[34]. Further undermining the attribution of safety assumed when an ADI is set, are the untested effects of the chemical. Dependent largely upon manufacturers to furnish data about the health effects of their chemicals, some experiments have simply not been done, leaving gaps in the toxicological profile. The US National Academy of Sciences has estimated that there is no data for 38% of pesticides, incomplete data for 52% and adequate safety data for only 10% of pesticides held by official bodies in the US[35]. Data gaps found by the Environmental Protection Agency (EPA) for lindane, for example, in 1985, included testing on acute inhalation, primary eye irritation, skin sensitivity, environmental fate studies and ecological effects[36].

Manufacturers of new pesticides in the UK must provide extensive data for registration for use and many of them are under review, yet the long term health effects of many of these pesticides are unknown[37]. Whilst toxicological effects have been examined for pesticides in isolation, there is a resounding silence on the effects of feeding on the cocktail of pesticides that we consume regularly in our daily diet. Little research has been carried out on the effects of pesticide residues in food that has been processed and none on the effects of irradiation of residues in food. All of this presents the possibility of potentially dangerous chemical transformations in our food[38]. Such scientific critique and method leaves much to be desired in an appraisal of the safety of residues in our food. Indeed there is no simple and reliable key. Yet, by conveying a sense of scientific precision and unequivocal accuracy, this arbitrary evaluation is referred to, relied upon and defended by governments and industry alike in the evaluation and guardianship of the safety of our diet.

The chronic health effects of these chemicals is one of the most controversial areas of debate in scientific circles. Many pesticides are suspected of being carcinogenic, teratogenic and mutagenic[39] and concern has been expressed since the 1960s that the long term effects of pesticides may contribute to human cancer. Some scientists support the argument advocated by Professor Bruce Ames of the University of California that the quantities of pesticides found in food pose minimal risks compared to the effects from carcinogens present naturally in our environment and that most cancer is self inflicted through smoking and poor diet[40]. Others, like Professor Samuel

Epstein of the University of Illinois, believe that the increase of synthetic carcinogens in our environment is causing today's high levels of cancer[41]. Whilst
programmes in the US have focused on the high fat content of diets promoting breast cancer, the biggest threat to women's health the world over,
researchers have not generally considered the effects of the contaminants in
food like organochlorine pesticides which become concentrated in fat.
Evidence from Israel, however, has indicated that the levels of breast cancer
dropped by 30% in women whose intake of organochlorine residues was low-
ered due to regulations reducing the levels of dieldrin and DDT in the diet[42].
The belief that there is no such thing as a safe dose of a carcinogen and that
one molecule may be enough to initiate cancer, is the basis of legislation in
the US called the Delaney Clause[43]. This stipulates that any chemical additives found to cause cancer in animals under test conditions should not be
allowed in human food. Pesticide residues however are exempt from this in
raw produce and some processed foods where the law requires that individual levels in these cases should be set to "protect public health whilst at the
same time taking into consideration the need for an adequate, wholesome
and economical food supply". The EPA has interpreted this to mean that it
must weigh cancer risk against economic considerations[44]. The EPA sanctions pesticide residue levels of a single carcinogenic pesticide on a single
food item at a level posing a 'negligible cancer risk' of 1 in 100,000 excess
cancers, which is equivalent to 35 excess deaths a year. Yet, extrapolating
this principle to a selection of 30 items of food containing 30 residues would
result in around 30,000 excess cancer deaths annually. Research from the
National Academy of Sciences has already conservatively associated some
20,000 excess deaths a year in the US with the consumption of 28 carcinogenic pesticide residues commonly found in food[45]. Whilst there is debate
and a lack of scientific or legislative consensus worldwide as to the carcinogenicity of various pesticides, the EPA has identified 66 potentially carcinogenic pesticides, all of which may legitimately be found in our food.

*Pesticides and Our Children*
The EPA's announcement in 1989 of their intention to withdraw the pesticide
alar after a proposed 18-month waiting period, coincided with the release of a

report entitled *Intolerable Risk: Pesticides in our Children's Food*[46]. Published by the Natural Resources Defense Council (NRDC), a New York-based pressure group, the report examined the potential effects of pesticide residues on children's health, finding them to be more vulnerable than adults to the health effects of pesticides. Looking at eight carcinogenic pesticides, NRDC estimated that children are four times as exposed to the pesticides examined than adults, as a result of eating proportionally more, relative to body weight, as well as eating much more fruit and vegetables, foods which are especially contaminated with pesticide residues. These two factors have not been taken into account when establishing safety levels for residues in the diet.

The report also drew attention to the fact that a child is likely to be more susceptible than adults to the toxicological effects of chemicals in their food. Children are likely to be highly sensitive to neurotoxic chemicals like organophosphate pesticides such as dichlorvos which affect the developing nervous system. Additionally, as a result of their bodies growing rapidly in infancy and early childhood, children are probably more vulnerable than adults to carcinogens which affect cell division. With evidence showing young children's bodies to be more susceptible to the toxic action of chemical compounds, the report provoked anxiety about the effects on children's development of a daily intake of these chemicals. Whilst the report has been criticised since, for errors which led to an over-estimate of the risks, the principles are still important. Indeed, a UK Government committee has expressed concern about the unknown potential effects of pesticide residues on children. Showing caution with the ADI and the MRL in food eaten by children, the UK Committee on Toxicology of Chemicals in the Environment recognised the difficulty in establishing the health risk to children from standard toxicological data and has urged a cautious approach in the evaluation of such hazards[47]. Such an attitude is all the more desirable; when cows' milk was judged by the Department of Health's Committee on Toxicity to be so heavily contaminated with dieldrin as to exceed the Codex ADI, the effect was said by MAFF's Working Party on Pesticide Residues to be "unknown"[48]. There is a further consideration — the cumulative effect of residues. Whilst the confectionery industry stringently defends its record of testing and the results obtained, those pesticide residues found in cocoa and chocolate are replicated throughout the whole of our diet. According to MAFF, lindane and DDE (a DDT metabolite) are the most commonly detected residues in our diet[49]. Through contamination of our food, lindane is contaminating our bodies with a significant presence in human fat and breast milk[50]. With a Codex ADI which has been set at 0.008 mg/kg body weight[51], lindane is considered to be both a possible carcinogen and a possible teratogen, causing birth defects. Lindane accumulates in the body and is stored in body fat where it builds up, although to a lesser degree than other organochlorines because it is metabolised fairly quickly in the body compared to other chemical compounds[52].

Evidence suggests that residues may react synergistically, with the great cocktail of chemicals that we are unconsciously consuming daily having a greater detrimental effect on our bodies when mixed together than they would as chemicals in isolation. Smoking and asbestos together cause greater rates of lung cancer than the sum of each individually, and synergistic reactions have been documented between organophosphate insecticides, but, as the synergistic effects of many chemicals remain untested, no-one knows if a combination of lindane, dieldrin and dichlorvos is more dangerous than lindane alone[53]. Lindane is considered by a global coalition of pesticide campaigners to be one of the 12 most dangerous pesticides used in the world and has been on the Pesticide Action Network's Dirty Dozen list which was launched in 1985 (see Fig 1.1, Chapter 7). Whilst not banned or restricted in food production in the UK, at least seven countries including Germany, the Netherlands, Japan and Singapore have totally banned the use of lindane and at least 16 others including the US, Canada, the Soviet Union, New Zealand and Denmark severely restrict its use (see Fig. 1.4 Chapter 7).

## The Circle of Poison

The presence of chemicals such as lindane in cocoa and chocolate in the UK and detected on cocoa entering the US[54], which are restricted-use chemicals in the Northern industrial nations, yet are exported and used on cocoa in the South, demonstrates what has become known as the 'Circle of Poison'. Environmentalists and health advocates have been lobbying hard to introduce legislation in the US to require importers and manufacturers to disclose the pesticides used in the production of imported raw materials. The 1990 US Farm Bill 'Circle of Poison' Amendment would have required importers of foods and commodities to certify annually "each pesticide chemical" used on that product by the producer. However, with the vociferous voice, amongst others, of the Chocolate Manufacturers' Association, the Amendment was removed from the Bill[55].

Finding residues of pesticides in chocolate should raise concern over the methods of production of cocoa and in particular the use of toxic agrochemicals to increase the crop yields, particularly when those chemicals are considered so dangerous they are banned elsewhere. Levels of residues in chocolate may not be considered harmful by industrialists and politicians, but they serve as an example of the ubiquitous presence of carcinogens in the food we consume daily. Fifty years ago our chocolate was free of organochlorine pesticide contamination (because these chemicals simply weren't used) and these chemicals do not need to be present in chocolate today. Whilst the presence of agrochemicals in our food, especially chemicals considered to be carcinogenic, calls the safety of our diet into question, science isdevoting little attention to these concerns, and governments continue to accept arbitrary standards of safety for public health. Rather than accept the rhetoric of safety from government and the agrochemical and food industries which justifies continued food contamination, we should consider the question of whether we need pesticides in our food at all.

**Figure 1**
PESTICIDE RESIDUES FOUND IN COCOA

| Residue | Possible Carcinogen | Possible Teratogen | Possible Mutagen |
|---|---|---|---|
| **organochlorine** | | | |
| ALDRIN[a] | * | * | * |
| DIELDRIN[a] | * | * | * |
| DDT[b] | * | | |
| ENDRIN[a] | * | * | * |
| HEPTACHLOR[b] | * | | |
| HEXACHLOROBENZENE | | | |
| LINDANE[a] | * | * | |
| | | | |
| **organophosphorus** | | | |
| DICHLORVOS[a] | * | * | * |
| MALATHION[a] | | * | |
| | | | |
| **carbamate** | | | |
| PROPOXUR[c] | * | | |
| | | | |
| INORGANIC BROMIDE | | | |

*Source of Residues in Cocoa:* BCCCA figures released in 1989
*Source of Pesticide Effects:*
a. Food Commission Report, Pesticides and Food - the need for real control,
b. Pesticides Action Network 'Dirty Dozen' pesticide fact sheets.
c. P is for Pesticides, Tim Lang and Charlie Clutterbuck, Ebury Press 1991 (citing EPA).

# *Realities*

# Land

The cocoa tree is a beautiful plant. Standing up to 40 foot tall, it is dwarfed by the tall coconut palms which provide it with shade from the sun. Its long, wide leaves are pale green and extend out from gnarled branches like fingers, which part to reveal long, yellow pods jutting out from the trunk and main arteries. It is the mass of dark beans held within the rich yellow pods which are valued as the essential ingredient of chocolate.

The tree flourishes in lowland tropical rainforest and grows within the tropical zone around the equator. From seed, the tree takes around eight years to reach maturity when it produces pinkish blooms which then form the large yellow pods which are cut and broken open for the beans.

There are several species of cocoa tree which have become identified in different regions. The Criollo tree is widely grown in the Americas. Although prone to disease, it is a tree which is noted for its delicate flavoured bean. The Forastero tree is more hardy and vigorous than the Criollo and the beans have a stronger flavour. It grows predominantly in Africa. These beans now form the greater part of all cocoa used in chocolate and have a reputation as the best quality cocoa beans on the market. A third tree, the Trinitario, was produced in the Caribbean when growers crossed the other two to produce a hybrid with a strong tasting bean which retains a fine flavour. This tree has since been taken to the cocoa growing regions of Asia.

Historically different regions have dominated the cocoa markets at different times, with the emphasis shifting from South America to the Caribbean in the 1800s, and then to West Africa throughout the 1900s. Today, with worldwide production at an all time high (see Table 4), South East Asia is striving to grow and out-produce all other regions.

Cash crop production has been viewed as a means to facilitate development, yet in striving to increase production, the damaging effects of such development are visible throughout the regions and take their toll on women and the land.

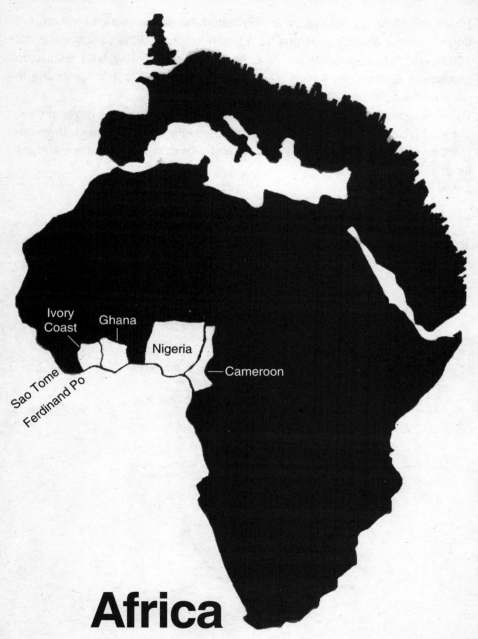

# WEST AFRICA

In the early 1800s, a handful of cocoa beans were purposefully carried from Bahia in Brazil to the Portuguese-held island of Sao Tome, off the coast of West Africa. As the Spanish had extended their interests westward during the previous centuries into the Americas, the Portuguese gained influence in Africa. They brought guns south to buy gold and grain and then later, as the Northern Europeans joined in the New World expansion, they took slaves. They sailed westward selling slaves to the expanding sugar, cocoa and coffee plantations and then returned home laden with wealth from the Americas. From its origins in the Spanish and Portuguese colonies in the New World, cocoa had regularly traversed the Atlantic on trading ships carrying all manner of South and Central American wealth home to Spain and Portugal. It was via the Portuguese trading routes that the exotic tree with a valuable fruit of one colony was introduced into the lands of another.

Cocoa has been an integral aspect of life in West Africa throughout this last century and has become an intrinsic part of the economies of the region. Ghana earns around 60% of its export exchange from this one crop[1] which covers over half of the available agricultural land in the country. One in four people earn their living from it here[2]. The Ivory Coast grows and exports mainly cocoa and coffee, producing one third of the world's cocoa at over 700,000 tonnes of beans in 1991[3] (see Table 5).

Millions of farmers throughout West Africa grow cocoa with techniques that have changed little over the last century. Yet these farmers over the same period have been involved in unprecedented political and economic changes as the local cocoa grower has become inextricably bound into the increasingly global economy. Spreading initially like wildfire, cocoa brought huge social changes in its wake as the local economy shifted into cash crop production for the outside world. Later, dependent upon the world market for income, fluctuating cocoa prices have placed the producers at the mercy of forces which they are unable to control, most noticeably during this last decade.

*The Arrival of a Cash Crop*

Cocoa arrived in Ghana shortly after the British assumed control and colonised. The Gold Coast was considered by the Europeans to be one of the richest territories in West Africa. The colonial government in the region was encouraging local farmers to produce exportable surplus and European entrepreneurs to invest and trade. Rubber was exported from the trees in the forests, and mining of gold, other minerals and diamonds increased as the government put in railways, roads and other infrastructure designed to facilitate export. As the transport links extended throughout the region, large areas of increasingly accessible rainforest were logged for timber.

Ghanaian farmers, previously growing a variety of food crops self-sufficiently, needed little encouragement into the cocoa economy. The first export of cocoa was made in 1891 and by 1910 the value of cocoa exceeded gold. By 1913 cocoa comprised half the annual exports of 5 million pounds[4]. This was reflected in the rapidly increasing imports of cocoa to the UK as the chocolate industry expanded. By 1915, Ghana[5] had become the world's biggest cocoa producer - a position it held until this last decade. The relationship between Britain and Ghanaian cocoa has remained strong, with Ghana exporting nearly one-third of its crop to the UK and supplying almost one-half of the UK's cocoa beans[6] (see Figure 2).

Ghanaian cocoa culture and that throughout West Africa generally consists of small farmers and share-croppers with most of the cocoa in Ghana produced on small plots of one to three acres. Although the men own the majority of the land which produces cocoa, the women are required to work to keep it productive. Men currently own around twice as much land as women and make up to 75% of all registered cocoa farmers[7]. Men have larger farms and are assisted on the farms by their wives, children and extended kin, though they are much less likely to assist if their wives own the farms. As throughout Africa, it is the women who also work to feed the family by farming food crops for the family to eat on the available space on the immature cocoa farms[8].

This inequitable access to land has not always been so. Colonial administration records indicate that it was the British, disregarding the possibility that women may wish to farm cocoa, who first limited their encouragement of cocoa growing to male heads of households[9]. Women did develop cocoa farms of their own accord, but they also assumed the role of family farm labourer in addition to that as the family's food provider, wife and mother.

Cocoa production gave men increasing autonomy, in contrast with women who were encouraged to work on the husband's farms. The changing economic and political emphasis towards valuing work which reaped financial income, resulted in women becoming increasingly marginalised as community leaders and political representatives[10]. Today the national union of agricultural workers is calling for the promotion of women's involvement in the union and the women themselves are appealing to the government for support in the face of the increasing threat to their inheritance of their husband's land, by increasing interference from other family members[11].

*A Quality Product*

Most cocoa is produced by farmers and smallholders with traditional techniques which sustain the reputation of Ghanaian cocoa as the best quality cocoa in the world. Farmers tend the land and the trees by weeding and pruning; they harvest the pods and dry the beans. Whilst the work on the farms is shared, men are more involved with felling and cultivating new land, planting cocoa and maintaining the farm. Women, in general, are responsible for weeding and for harvesting the cocoa crop - picking, collecting and breaking the pods.

Trees are grown from seed and then seedlings are planted out. They bloom with masses of small pink flowers after around 5 years and take around 8 years to reach full maturity, when some of the flowers will be fertilized and develop into yellow pods. Harvesting takes place in 2 seasons in the year when the pods are cut from the trees, broken open and the insides scooped out. The beans grow surrounded by a sweet, white, acidic mucilage which is then cleaned away. The beans are then placed in piles under banana leaves in the heat of the sun to ferment.

This is the procedure which turns the rather bitter raw cocoa bean into the rich ingredient of chocolate. After a couple of days under the leaves, the beans are raked out to dry in the sun, then they are bagged up and transported from the farm to the local storage depot to begin the process of sale and transportation which usually results in the beans being bought by cocoa processing and confectionery companies and being shipped to Europe and the US.

As they have done since before the end of the colonial era, when they sold direct to trading and buying agents, farmers bring their bagged cocoa to the local village storehouse, where it is weighed and checked for quality. These days this is done by the local government buyers.

The Cocoa Marketing Board, locally known as the Cocobod, was set up by the colonial government in 1947, 10 years after government first centralised cocoa buying and selling arrangements, and still operates today The Cocobod is a centralised marketing administration which guarantees to buy all the cocoa produced by the farmers for a fixed price. The government then stores and transports the cocoa selling it on to the world market.

As well as taking responsibility for the purchase of all cocoa, it also provides agricultural support services such as pesticide spraying, runs cocoa plantations and undertakes research into crop development. Whilst the farmers have a guaranteed buyer, they are unable to negotiate the price.

*Political and Economic Changes*

For many decades the Cocobod oversaw the expansion of the Ghanaian cocoa industry which, in a time of increasing production worldwide, maintained its position as the world's leading producer from the 1900s. This situation however, has changed over the last 20 years. Under the leadership of the enigmatic Kwame Nkrumah, Ghana was the first African nation to gain independence in 1957. Hailed as the Black Star of Africa, Nkrumah was eager to move Ghana away from its dependence on cash crops for the old colonial markets. He promoted self sufficiency through industrialisation.

His visions of independence for the African nations, however, failed to materialise as his plans and schemes pushed the country increasingly into debt - half a billion US$ by 1966[12]. Nine years after his election, he was overthrown in a coup, and Ghanain government has been punctuated with six successive coups since then.

During the 1970s when cocoa was receiving a good price on the international market and politicians spent fortunes on military hardware and lavish travels, the cocoa farmer was receiving little reward. The farmers resorted to planting food crops in order to feed themselves when credit notes remained unpaid; crops were not harvested and, as cocoa trees reached the end of their lives, were not replaced. By 1983, cocoa production had fallen to around 150,000 tonnes a year[13].

From its position as the world's largest cocoa producer, with staggering outputs of over 600,000 tonnes of cocoa a year around the mid 1960s, the cocoa output has reflected Ghana's economic decline. By the early 1980s, cocoa production had dropped to a quarter of this[14] and Ghana had fallen from first place in the world cocoa producing stakes to third (see Table 5).

The last decade has seen attempts to counteract the economic decline which have brought praise from the Western economic institutions, although the methods used have brought increasing hardship to the people. Flight Lieutenant Jerry Rawlings, after leading an initial coup in 1979 was popularly reinstated by the people in 1981, with policies to revitalise the cocoa industry and implement economic change.

*The World Bank, IMF and SAPs*

Threatened with bankruptcy, he embraced the World Bank and the International Monetary Fund (IMF)[15], and a major programme of rehabilitation of the cocoa industry commenced within a full scale programme of major economic change. To deal with the debt and to fund Ghana's economic regeneration, Rawlings drew vast loans from these agencies, making Ghana the third biggest borrower in the world by 1988. Such loans entail the compulsory imposition of structural adjustment programmes (SAPs), which are designed to make the country borrowing money more attractive to foreign investment, thus promoting the expansion of global free trade. SAPs demand cost-cutting measures, aiming to increase competitiveness on the world market. These measures include cutting social services, devaluation of currency, privatisation of state-owned industry, promotion of foreign private investment and the reduction of public expenditure through large scale lay-offs of state employees. Over US$3 billion of IMF, World Bank and money from other sources, such as the British Government, has been poured into Ghana since the ambitious programme of economic reform was instigated in 1983 and, as exports are now rising, the country has been viewed by world bankers as a shining success story. Since 1983 the economy has grown by 6% pa, and inflation has dropped from triple digit figures to less than 20%[16].

Yet even the bankers who implement the austere penny pinching policies recognise them to be detrimental to many citizens as the rush to promote economic growth takes precedence over the social and humanitarian needs of the people and the sustainable future of the environment.

Cocoa production has been heavily promoted by the World Bank as part of the package of loans. In order to encourage the farmers to return to growing this crop, they were guaranteed half the price offered on the world market by the Cocobod, which initially amounted to a four-fold pay increase. At the end of 1989 they were receiving US$37 for a 60 kg sack[17]. More land was planted with cocoa trees in the mid-1980s and derelict farms left in the 1970s were resurrected, so that, by 1987, half of Ghana's cultivated land was covered with cocoa.

However, rather than retaining traditional labour-intensive practices, the Bank is promoting capital-intensive practices which require the use of chemicals and machines, arguing that this is the way to cultivate and produce cocoa more cost-effectively[18]. Whilst demanding that Cocobod subsidies for pesticides, fertilizers and tools be cut, a 1988 package (worth US$120 million) was spent on the extension services to farmers, offering machinery, chemicals, training and higher-yielding varieties, much of which must be imported from northern industrial nations[19].

Farmers and the agricultural workers union have been resisting such demands, which entail fundamental changes in the way of life, as people are made redundant in the new technological process and farmers become dependent on having currency to pay for the technology[20.] In an effort to emulate the expansion of the industry in South East Asia, where cocoa is grown primarily on large privately-owned monocultural plantations, the Cocobod has been encouraged to restructure its 6,400 hectares of plantations. In response to the Bank's demand for private investment, 52 of the 92 Cocobod plantations have now been sold off to private investors[21]. Whilst being able to produce greater quantities of cocoa more cheaply, such a trend may also threaten the cocoa quality, which is considered inferior when grown under such mass conditions.

*Social Implications*
The social costs of adjustment are visible throughout the country as the wholesale acceptance of Western economic systems has undermined the old sustainable way of life and created new dependency and poverty. Such developments have provoked and necessitated further World Bank schemes like PAMSCAD, the full name of which - Programme of Action to Mitigate the Social Consequences of Adjustment - is self-explanatory[22]. The shocking fall in food self-sufficiency from 98% in the late 1960s to 8% today has escalated poverty[23] and malnutrition is estimated to affect half the rural poor. Food prices have risen dramatically; a loaf of bread now costs more than a day's work[24]. IMF policies have accelerated the decline of social health care and education structures, as emphasis is placed on upgrading roads and railways to make it easier to transport and export increasing quantities of cocoa, timber and gold to the West.

Women suffer most from deteriorating social infrastructure with their dual role as workers and carers for the family. With reduced health services, they spend more time looking after the sick. The pressure to produce crops for export reduces the availability of food for home consumption and women are forced seek work at any wage in order to buy food for their families.

Stringent economies imposed by the World Bank are applied nationwide to facilitate increased cocoa production at reduced cost, but the price on the world market controlled by Western commodity dealers has plummeted over the last 10 years. The amount of cocoa beans produced by the Ghanains has doubled in the last few years since the floor of 1983, to almost 300,000 tonnes in 1990, yet in the last decade the price paid for one tonne has dropped to half the value it was then[25].

*The Paradox of Debt*
Commodity prices and debt have been the two most profoundly detrimental economic influences upon developing nations over the last decade, and the two are not unrelated. Part of the explanation for the paradoxical circumstances of growers increasing cocoa output in the face of massive overproduction is, according to Third World observers - the debt[26]. Third World debt currently stands at around US$1.3 trillion for 1990[27]. In seeking repayment,

and providing further loans, these international institutions are imposing their stringent SAPs for "export oriented growth strategy". As a result cocoa growers have pushed on with increasing the harvest at a time when cocoa was being stockpiled rather than consumed.

Such policies, have ensured the high output of cash crops and has contributed to the mountains of cocoa beans, coffee beans, tea leaves and other basic raw materials piled in warehouses in the North resulting inthe dramatic drop in price. Whilst both the IMF and the World Bank claim to tailor their loans and SAPs to fit each country, the Bank has been criticised for its uncoordinated development policy which has resulted in indiscriminate expansion of the same products from countries which are in direct competition for the same commodity markets[28]. The World Bank's own figures show that while countries undergoing adjustment programmes have increased their exports, any benefit has been negated as a result of the deterioration in the terms of trade (i.e. the relationship of value of exports to cost of imports). Now implemented across much of the developing world, it is these SAPs which have led to so much damage to the environment, the poor and in particular the women of these regions[29].

Developing countries being dependent on one sole crop are especially vulnerable with current mainstream economic thinking which demands that this established resource be further exploited and exported to earn income and repay debt. As Frances Moor Lappe and Joseph Collins state in Food First in 1980[30] ' one of the most oppressive myths is that underdeveloped countries can grow only 'tropical crops', and that they should exploit this natural advantage by exporting them. This is the case particularly with many of the African nations where for example Uganda relies on coffee for 95% of its export earnings, as Ghana relies on cocoa for 59%. Now, whilst Ghana's cocoa exports have doubled since the early 80s, so has the debt, which in 1990 was an estimated US$3 billion[31]. For Ghana, the effect of the falling commodity price has been devastating.

Farmers continue to cultivate cocoa because it is considered by the people to be their inheritance. Even in the face of the lowest prices for ten years, farmers maintain their farms. They are diversifying into other food crops which reap higher prices and which feed themselves. When everyone was self-sufficient in food, maize, plantain and coyocam had little cash value. Today, however, when few people now grow their own food, the farmers are able to sell these for profit[32]. Such is the legacy of development that food is now readily available in the markets, but not all can afford to buy it.

Termed 'maldevelopment' by the ecofeminist writer Vandana Shiva, Western-style development, encouraged by governments and imposed by the economic institutions is revealing itself to be a damaging course of action for the majority. Encouraging dependence on cash crops away from food production has resulted in people struggling to feed themselves, whilst expected returns from selling the crop on the global market have turned to dust. The benefits of West Africa's cash crop expansion continue to accrue to the Northern nations.

CARIBBEAN

Mexico

Columbia

Ecuador

BRAZIL

Bahia

Rondonia

# The Americas

# BRAZIL

Cocoa thrives in the tropical regions of most of the Caribbean and Central and South America. The coastal region of Chiapas in Mexico and western Guatemala supplied the Maya and then the Aztecs for centuries. The Spanish, eager to expand their supply of valuable beans, extended the cocoa growing region with plantations throughout Guatemala into Salvador. By the time that Europe had become a large market for cocoa in the mid 1600s, cocoa production had moved into South America, and the Central American cocoa growing regions had declined. Today, only scattered groves along the pacific coastal plain serve as a reminder of the former greatness of the Cacao coast of Central America[1].

Mass production of cocoa boomed in Venezuela and Ecuador. As the Spanish, Dutch and English set up cocoa, sugar and coffee plantations in the 1600s using slave labour brought from Africa, the Caribbean islands also began to grow the crop. Venezuela later turned its cocoa land to coffee production, but Ecuador, Colombia and the Dominican Republic continue to produce plenty of cocoa today.

Initially taking the cocoa from the wild stands of cocoa trees in the Amazon basin, the Portuguese began to export cocoa from Brazil in the 1700s. The first plantations of cocoa trees were planted in the Bahia region in North East Brazil from where exports began in the 1830s. By the turn of the century exports from plantations were greater than the wild cocoa picked from the rainforest.

Unlike West Africa, cocoa in Brazil has always been grown predominantly on large plantations in a system which originates from the time of colonisation, when large areas of land were handed out to individuals as settlements from the Crown. As now, the plantation economy was dominated by the landowning aristocracy who owned the estates. Many new landowners converted the land to sugar plantations as the increasingly sweet tooth of the Europeans ensured hefty profits. Many others cleared land for rubber.

After independence in the second half of the 19th century, the land was taken on by the native creole population, who maintained the rubber and sugar plantations with bonded labour and later expanded the cocoa planta-

71

tions. Huge tracts of land in the north eastern coastal state of Bahia were planted with cocoa during the early 1900s and cocoa production expanded rapidly, rising from 3,000 tonnes around the turn of the century to 60,000 tonnes by 1920[2].

Cocoa production has increased five-fold since that time and Brazil is now the world's second largest producer exporting 270,000 tonnes in 1990. Of this output 90% is concentrated in Bahia, where an area the size of Netherlands is devoted to cocoa production[3] Cocoa is now increasingly grown in the Amazon region and 100,000 hectares of new plantations have been planted so far[4]. Brazil has also developed a processing and manufacturing industry to make cocoa products and chocolate.

*Industrial Development*

Brazil has undertaken a major revolution during the last 25 years as it has embraced industrial development. Having borrowed heavily from the World Bank and other lenders during the 1970s to invest in manufacturing, economic indicators suggest the country has made a successful transition into the industrialised world with 6.4% growth in economy and a US$18 billion trade surplus in 1985. Brazil ranks 7th in steel production, 9th in machinery production and was the 11th largest car producer in the world by the mid 1980s[5]. However, Brazil currently has a debt running at US$111 million so by 1988, 35% of all export exchange flowed back to the North as debt repayment[6].

In order to fund such development, the country has exploited its major resource - the land. With the emphasis on increasing production for export, farmers were urged to grow more cash crops. The large landholdings have expanded at the expense of smallholdings and rainforest. The government has encouraged the foreign transnationals into the region with tax incentives, cheap labour and cheap land.

Agribusiness expanded in Brazil with an array of agricultural operations from soya production to beef farming. As a result, by the 1980s, Brazil had become the world's biggest coffee, sugar and orange producer, the second largest cocoa and soya producer and the third largest maize producer as well as producing significant amounts of cotton, rice, cereals and tobacco.

In 1990 Brazil exported 270,000 tonnes of cocoa, and was the world's second largest cocoa producer (see Table 5). Whilst there are still a number of farmers producing cocoa on smallholdings, encouraged by the government and Western models of economic development and crop production, cocoa production is dominated by the estates with four-fifths of all cocoa now grown on plantations[7].

The land is becoming increasingly concentrated into the hands of the large estate owners, as they buy up the lands of the smaller producers and convert their smallholdings to plantation. One person may own as many as 40 or 50 estates, over half of which will be 200 hectares or more. As the land is converted to monoculture, over 15% of the cocoa growing land in Bahia is now organised as estates of more than 1000 hectares[8].

Such disparity in land ownership has bought violence in its wake as smallholders have been thrown off their land. Land struggle is not new to the cocoa growing regions in Brazil; in the 1920s the cocoa barons sought to expand their lands to take advantage of the then high prices for cocoa. But violence has escalated in the cocoa region as throughout Brazil in recent times, as the smallholders have been forced to give up their land altogether[9].

This economic development and redistribution of land has led to a massive displacement of the population from a rural to urban society. In 1965 half the population lived a rural life; by 1985 73% of the people lived in an urban environment. Images of urban life, are all too often of urban slums on the outskirts of sprawling cities and both poverty and landlessness are huge problems facing Brazil today[10]. The cost of cash crop production is high for the people who have become the dispossessed in their own land.

*Working Conditions*

Cheap labour is fundamental to today's Brazilian plantation economy and has been of major significance since the time of the Portuguese. While slavery was outlawed a century ago, today people working on the plantations under poor conditions receive meagre reward and have few other options available to them. Today around 200,000 people work on the cocoa estates in Bahia[11]. While both women and men work on the plantations, women are paid half of a man's wage for the same work and children receive even less.

Women workers earn around US$25 a month[12]. Increasingly, work is done on contract and paid by the task, but wages for piecework may not meet daily living expenses and children have to work to complete quotas. Women planting out saplings onto cleared land receive US$1 per 100[13] and would be unable to buy a kilo of meat with a whole day's pay[14].

The conditions of life as a worker are bereft. With unemployment currently running at around 250,000 in Bahia[15], little is available for those who come from the towns each week looking for work. For those lucky enough to get a contract, transport is not available so the workers can walk up to three hours to reach the plantation, bringing food and a mat to sleep on for the duration of the contract and then walk home again at the end of the work[16]. Crowded together in the urban sprawl, social provisions are beyond the reach of many of these people, where school is available only for a minority of children, medical care is scarce and malnutrition is widespread[17].

For those who live on the estate, the plantation is all-encompassing. Permanent workers live on the estate with their families in small wooden houses and are able to raise a few animals, pick fruit and sometimes plant vegetables. Yet they receive the lowest pay of all the plantation workers, diminishing these benefits. Over the last few years there have been increasing numbers of evictions of families, as the plantation owners seek to reduce their ties and responsibilities to their workforce. In 1972, permanent wage earners accounted for around 72% of all workers with 28% on temporary contracts; today the situation is likely to be reversed as the estates reduce their overheads and commitments[18].

*The Oppression of Women*

Conditions are poor for many of the agricultural workers in Brazil, but women working both in agriculture and industry find that, as well as earning less, they are facing further profoundly discriminatory conditions. Women may lose their jobs when they become pregnant; at the Garotto chocolate factory in Espirito Santo State twelve women were sacked in 1989 despite the support of the trade union and adverse local publicity[19].

The most oppressive discriminatory condition applied to women seeking work both on plantations and in the industrial sector is the demand for proof of sterilisation before a woman can get a contract or is hired for a job[20]. Previously, women seeking work were asked to supply pregnancy tests before being given a job. In 1987, the IMF demanded that Brazil reduce its population as a condition for credit on debt repayment and following the extension of maternity leave from 90 to 120 days, employers are now readily asking for sterilisation papers. Sterilisation of women is now reaching massive proportions. Health Ministry information shows that more than 300,000 women are being sterilised each year and by 1990 more than seven million women had had the operation[21]. In some of the provinces of the North East, 71% of women of child-bearing age are sterilised[22]. Such figures serve to demonstrate the disempowerment of women who must denounce their ability to bear children in order to have a job.

Although many of the workers in the chocolate factories are women[23], by comparison, few union leaders are female and women's concerns and issues have had little voice. However, women's wages were an issue of debate in 1988, which, together with the sacking of the pregnant women, resulted in union action and public attention. Women today are becoming increasingly active in the traditionally male dominated unions and are drawing women's issues to union attention. Similarly, the major concerns of the women in agricultural trade unions are the demands for equal pay, the rights for a woman not to lose her job when she becomes pregnant and for a woman to be employed without a certificate of sterilization[24].

*The Influence of Transnationals*

Some transnational companies involved in the chocolate industry have a strong presence in Brazil. Those workers and trade union representatives who have had a chance to compare conditions between processing and manufacturing factories in Brazil and those in the industrial nations know that conditions in Brazil are poor by comparison.

Reports by the Amsterdam based Transnational Information Exchange (TIE)[25], demonstrate the disparity of working conditions in the North and South. Cargill is a North American corporation with a large involvement in cocoa processing and currently processes around 90,000 tonnes of cocoa a year, some at its plant in Brazil. Cargill's plants in the Netherlands and Brazil demonstrate the discrepancy of wages between North and South, where, according to TIE, whilst the Brazilian cost of living is around three-quarters of that in the Netherlands, the Brazilians are receiving only one-tenth of the wages of the Dutch.

Nestlé, the European-based transnational corporation with a huge presence in Brazil, operates a cocoa processing plant in the Bahia region and a chocolate manufacturing factory near Sao Paolo. Nestlé workers' claim disparity in working conditions in Brazil compared with other countries. The workers also expressed their concerns to TIE about health and safety and sexual discrimination in promotion as well as pay.

The trade union president of a factory owned by Joanes S.A., the largest cocoa processing company in Brazil which is owned by British-based E. D. & F. Mann, visited the latter's British Cocoa Mills at Hull in 1992. He saw British workers doing the same job as he and his colleagues in Brazil, and was struck by their better working conditions[26].

The cocoa cash crop grown predominantly to be exported to the North, displays the inequity of centuries of disadvantage applied by landowners to workers, women particularly. The poor conditions and low pay, also reflect the disparity displayed by transnational companies as they implement lower standards in their processing and manufacturing operations than are acceptable at home. Now, plantation workers with no land on which to grow their own cocoa or their own food are fully dependent upon receiving an income in order to survive.

Yet although the economic success of the large cocoa plantations relies on the use of pesticides and of cheap labour, the cocoa price is currently so low that some growers have decided that the wood of the cocoa tree is more valuable than the fruit and are unwilling to continue its production at all[27].

South
East Asia

PHILIPPINES

PAPUA
NEW
GUINEA

Irian
Jaya

MALAYSIA

Singapore

Kalimantan

Sumatra

INDONESIA

# MALAYSIA

Long before cocoa was taken south to the African regions, it had been carried westward along the developing trading routes to the East. From Acapulco to Manila, cocoa beans were transported across the Pacific by the Spanish who had colonised the Philippines in the 16th century. Cocoa was then carried and cultivated through Indonesia and across South East Asia, reaching Sri Lanka and India by the 1700s. However, it was not until very recently that cocoa was grown in the region as a commercial crop for export. Unsuccessful attempts were made to grow cocoa in Malaysia earlier this century, but it was only in the 1970s that the venture was fruitful and success has brought rapid expansion; production has expanded four-fold in the last 10 years, with Malaysia now the largest producer in the region and the fourth largest producer in the world (see Table 5). Following this pattern of intensive cash crop expansion which is repeated throughout the region, the countries of South East Asia strive for economic development.

Cocoa is the third most prolific cash crop in Malaysia. The first plantations to be established, by the Europeans during the late 18th century, grew coffee, tea and sugar. Later, with the discovery of tin and the first rubber plantations established in the middle of the 19th century, large numbers of labourers were brought in from southern China and India by the colonists. Initially, work was especially heavy as vast areas of remote rainforest was cleared to make space for the plantations. Living in sordid and unhealthy conditions, around 1 in 12 workers died from malaria, tuberculosis, cholera and malnutrition[1].

*Life on the Plantation*

Today 250,000 plantation workers, more than half of them women[2], continue to live in poverty and suffer ill health. Since being brought over from India by the British, Tamils continue to be the predominant working population on the plantations[3] where little has changed in working conditions over the last 150 years.

The plantations extend over mile upon mile of planted land intersected by red, dusty roads leading through thick rows of oil palm trees and the more delicate cocoa trees, often grown on the same estate. Plantations are run like prisons; landscape and lifestyle are uniform and monotonous. For an outsider, entering a plantation is a precarious affair, with gun carrying security guards checking people in and out. For the workers, it is a life of restriction. Most work on the palm oil and rubber plantations but around 3% of the workforce work on the more recently developed cocoa plantations[4]. Life is regimented by the endless work, beginning with a bell and roll call at 6.30 am.

On the cocoa plantations, where the workers are predominantly women fulfilling the additional duties of wife and housekeeper, the day begins at 4.30 am, when they get up to make breakfast for the whole family, to prepare lunch and get the younger children to school. To miss roll call is to forfeit a day's pay as the jobs are assigned at this time and the general workers spend the morning either in the nursery attending to new plants or harvesting the pods. Those assigned to spraying pesticides spend the whole day walking with a sprayer on their back.

In the afternoon the workers, sitting on the ground, break open the pile of harvested cocoa pods, scoop out the beans and place them in sacks. New workers soon learn not to eat too much of the sticky sweet mucilage which protects the beans. This highly acidic substance is soon felt painfully in the stomach. There is little protection, however, against its corrosive action on the hands. At the end of the long working day, around 4 pm, the workers wait by the side of the tracks through the plantation for the arrival of the sector manager, who, with a crude pair of weighing scales, will weigh up the day's labour and determine the wages due.

The women who work in Selangor River on the Peninsula Malaysia earn 12 Malaysian cents for each kilo of beans harvested. Able to pick an average 120 kg a day, the women receive around M$14.40 (around £3.20) for a day's work. They work 26 days each month and, at such poor wages, cannot afford to miss a day. Nevertheless, to be sick is to lose pay, to pick less than 85 kg will automatically disqualify the worker from any basic salary and the plantations will not operate or pay wages when it rains[5].

With a monthly income of around M$300 (about £60), this salary will not adequately support a family. The joint income of husband and wife leaves little after purchasing their simple diet of rice and vegetables and any essential sundries. Housing, allocated by the estate, consists of row upon row of basic units inhabited by large, extended families. Some have continuous electricity and water supplies; many do not. Many people live and sleep together in the overcrowded, compartmentalised conditions of the sparsely furnished rooms. A recent survey[6] drew public attention to the conditions of the estate workers with shocked headlines in the press[7]. Most estates do not provide clean water; 41% of all toilet facilities do not meet basic standards and most housing is substandard. In the corner of each living room, however, stands the icon of Western accomplishment and beacon of American propaganda - the television and video. But, costing M$3 (about 60p) to hire a video for a night, it is expensive and ill-afforded.

Since the 1950s, women plantation workers have received equal pay. Yet, like women throughout the world, they are responsible for double duty as income earner and also housekeeper and mother. Large families of six or seven children are common on the plantations, where less than a quarter of the estates provide family planning services[8]. Women's health issues are generally ignored and health care is minimal. It is usual for women who are eight months pregnant to work and miscarriages occur regularly under the burden of continued heavy labour.

Sexual harassment is a further occupational hazard experienced by many of the women on the plantations. On the estates where the socio-cultural atmosphere demands that these experiences be covered up and denied, investigation by Sahabat Alam Malaysia (Friends Of The Earth Malaysia) has revealed that the extent of the problem is even wider than the frequent reports of molestation and rape suggest[9]. Options for women are limited. As only men are accorded head of household status, eligible for such benefits as accommodation, women are without practical access to independence on the estates.

Few plantation workers are aware of their rights to better conditions, health and safety information and better wages. It is left to grass roots campaigners to promote awareness amongst the workers of these issues. Poisoning by paraquat is increasingly used as a premature exit from a seemingly endless arduous existence[10].

If anything, living standards are declining, as levels of pay, negotiated every five years, have not kept up with inflation[11]. Ironically, while the prosperous classes of Malaysia have developed enough to make them an attractive new market for Western chocolate manufacturers, the plantation labourers have experienced a continued decline in living standards, and are as unlikely as ever to taste a bar of chocolate.

Some workers are beginning to see a way out, if not for themselves, then at least for their children. Aware that, whilst their own lives will probably continue in the same way without respite, some of the women anticipate that their daughters will be able to leave for a better future. In this case, that generally means the electronics factories in the industrialising regions, which have burgeoned over the last decade and where wages are higher but the quality of life is, arguably, as poor.

*Economic Expansion*

Malaysia is attempting a major transformation, within just 20 years of economic expansion, to emerge into the glorified ranks of the industrial world. With a GDP per person of over US$2000 in 1989, compared to say US$350 in Ghana, it was recently termed by the World Bank as having 'upper middle income' of the 'less developed countries'[12]. With the 'newly industrialised countries' (NICs), Hong Kong, Korea, Taiwan and Singapore, for neighbours setting examples of 'success', Malaysia is going all out for Western models of development. In these terms it is succeeding, with economic growth in 1989 of 8.5% and over M$5 billion in foreign investment in the same year.

Eager to propel itself toward NIC status, vast sums of money have been invested in the manufacturing sector, giving rise to an industrial boom in areas such as electronics, chemicals and textiles. Industrial zones have grown on the peninsular expanding urban development and creating factory jobs[13]. Despite the industrial drive, the country is highly dependent upon cash crop agriculture to provide foreign exchange. Agriculture provided one-quarter of export earnings, one-fifth of the GNP and one-third of the employment in 1990[14].

*Opening Up the Land*

Expansion of all cash crop output has been facilitated by the Government's eagerness to follow the process of "opening up the land"[15]. Plantation development, like mining, is an exploitative conversion of rainforest land to consumable resource. Indeed, agro-conversion is the biggest cause of deforestation in Peninsula Malaysia where it has proceeded at a rapid rate since the turn of the century. By 1980 the area under permanent crops was 11 times higher than in 1910 and agricultural conversion is estimated to account for 90% of the 90,000 hectares deforested since 1976[16].

Cocoa is Malaysia's third biggest cash crop, earning the country US$448 million in 1990, and undergoing the biggest expansion of all crops throughout the 1980s. The amount of land devoted to cocoa expanded to 420,000 hectares and the Malaysian Economic Fourth Plan from 1981-85 was known as 'The Era of Cocoa Development', as exports jumped from 30,000 tonnes in 1980 to 260,000 tonnes a decade later[17].

This took place most rapidly in the state of Sabah on the northern region of the island of Borneo, which now produces over half Malaysia's cocoa crop. Around one-eighth of the land logged in Sabah has been converted to the cocoa crop and expansion is set to continue[18]. The Primary Industries Minister has expressed his support for the "expansion of cultivation of plantation crops suited to Sarawak and Sabah - land where primary agricultural potential is still available"[19]. The Government's Sixth Malaysia Plan, anticipates a further 7% increase in the total cocoa acreage in Malaysia by 1995, as yet more rainforest is logged and converted to cocoa in Sabah[20].

Plantations, believed to be more cost effective than smallholdings have been encouraged by the government, eager to increase productivity which has now reached 1000 kg of beans produced per hectare of land[21]. This is vast compared to the West African smallholder who produces around 250 kg per hectare[22]. Around 55% of Malaysia's cocoa is currently produced on plantation. Eight or nine plantation companies account for the majority of cash crop production in the country. Many of these were initially established last century by the colonials and remained British-owned after independence in 1955, until the 1980s when the Government, pushing its policy of 'Malaysianisation', pressed for home ownership of these primary industries.

Sime Darby, Guthrie, United Plantations are colonial companies whose names, displayed throughout the plantation region on the borders of their estate territory, are firmly established in the national psyche. These companies continue to profit from the export of the three major cash crop commodities. However, as the world market prices fall and these commodities become less profitable, the recent trend for the plantation companies has been diversification into other areas of business such as manufacturing, oil, and property. Falling prices notwithstanding, cash crops continue to provide profits, especially when land is cheap[23].

Undeterred by the diminishing value of the crop, large areas of land have been converted in recent years to produce cocoa, as the government, bent on economic development is determined to compete for a stake in the world market. Now with over half of the crop produced on Sabah, and the majority of Malaysian cocoa grown on the large highly productive monocultural plantations, the Malaysian output is feeding the world surplus and the price continues to fall.

*Resettlement into a Cash Economy*

As well as the expansion of the plantation sector, the government is also involved in encouraging the development of cash crops on smallholdings. Smallholders continue to produce 45% of the crop on small plots of land of one or two hectares located predominantly on the Peninsular Malaysia and increasingly on Sarawak. Owning their land and tending the crops themselves, the smallholders often intercrop the cocoa with coconuts and also plant food for their families.

While most of the cocoa land in Sabah is held in private estate ownership, the government land authority (FELDA) plays a major role in land development in Sarawak, where most of the new cocoa producing smallholdings are located. The government has been involved in transmigration and land development schemes, implementing their policy of 'urbanisation of rural areas'. This means moving the indigenous people who live by subsistence cultivation and establishing them as smallholders or as members of a 'nucleus estate plantation', where they contribute crops grown on their land to a larger central pool - the nucleus. Such schemes have been funded by the government and the World Bank throughout the last decade[24].

The major precept for the Government migration programme is poverty alleviation. The rationale that cash crop production will increase foreign exchange earnings and people will benefit from having a cash income has motivated the Government to move families into forest land at a cost of M$55,000 (£ 10,000) per family. This has resulted in the resettlement of 26,000 families and the conversion of 300,000 hectares of land to cash crops in the last five years. In total, over 700,000 people had been resettled by the end of 1990[25].

Production has indeed increased, but communities have been accelerated into a cash oriented economy and they have become dependent upon obtaining money from the crops they grow in order to eat. Unlike the forest which previously supplied all their needs, emergency food supplies have had to be flown into such sites on several occasions[26].

A study on women who were resettled with their families to grow cocoa in the Batang Ai region of Sarawak, indicated that the resettlement had created concerns and presented new hardship. For the women, speaking about their new way of life, such development has curtailed their rights and freedoms and increased their insecurity. They have expressed their fears at the new dependence upon money which is required for all provisions. As the new land title is awarded to the newly defined 'head of the household', who is always male, women have lost their rights to the land. Women stated that one of their biggest concerns is that the overriding need to plant cocoa has denied them land on which they can plant paddy, as they had done before as a spiritual rite which reaffirmed their link with their land. Such resettlement and forced conversion into the cash economy has entailed for these women a sense of deprivation and insecurity[27]. The starkest irony is that the price they receive for their hard grown crop is now less than the cost of production.

The Government's hopes of poverty alleviation are meaningless beside the current price paid for the crop. The December 1989 price for cocoa dipped to US$1,900 a tonne - one-third less than the smallholder's costs of production estimated at US$2,800 a tonne in 1990. Government figures judge one in six smallholders to be living below the poverty line[28] and they are being advised by the Smallholder Association to take up poultry farming and fruit trees until the price improves. In desperation however, 10,000 smallholders have already destroyed their cocoa trees on the Peninsular in the hope that another crop will be more profitable[29].

**Chocolate Unwrapped** The Politics of Pleasure

The government remains committed to continued expansion of cash crop production to ensure greater exports. Indeed, sustained increases in income from exports are now essential to fuel the 'economic miracle', as around one-quarter of this income goes to service the national debt, which reached around US$18 million in 1985.

Similarly, plantations, are currently unable to make any money from cocoa and some are beginning to convert to oil palm in the hope of improved income. According to one estate manager, 1 tonne of cocoa cost US$3000 to produce and, at the April 1992 price of US$2600 a tonne, was losing money. His advice was for Westerners to eat more chocolate to raise the price. However, to follow his advice is to perpetuate the cycle of cash crop dependency.

# INDONESIA

Indonesia has also been implementing strategies for development since the 1970s, with assistance from the World Bank. To fund thes and to counterbalance the loss of earnings from the fall in the price of oil, Indonesia has expanded cash crop cultivation. As the fifth most populous country on earth, with 177 million people, most of whom are living on the main islands of Java and Madura, the Government has also sought to counter the demographic disparity by relocating families from the overcrowded centres out to the less populous islands of Sumatra, Kalimantan (Borneo) and Irian Jaya. Originally resettling people as self-sufficient rice farmers, the Government has recently been relocating these people at great social cost onto estate projects to grow cash crops including cocoa.

Cocoa has been an attractive crop since it received high prices on the world market at the end of the 1970s, and the Indonesian Government has been encouraging its production throughout the 1980s, despite its recent fall in value. Cocoa production has increased eight-fold over the last decade, at a rate even greater than that of Malaysia, to reach 130,000 tonnes by 1990 (see Table 5), and the Government is seeking to double production by the end of the century. Current plans are to expand the cocoa estates especially on Sulawesi and Kalimantan, estimated by the World Bank to be the largest ever tree crop investment worth around US$5 billion[1].

At first, cocoa was predominantly grown on plantation estates begun under Dutch colonisation, with attendant poor working conditions reflecting those in Malaysia. With workers still only receiving less than US$1 a day (and women only three quarters of that figure) and land so cheap, the Government believes that it can grow the crop more cheaply than anyone else[2]. A new strategy to further increase production has been recently implemented to link cash crop production with the vast transmigration schemes which are relocating people to the outer regions.

*Transmigration*

Considering it to be the solution to over-population and the increasing poverty in the densely populated centres of the main islands, a transmigration programme has been operating on a huge scale since 1979. Throughout the early 1980s, the Government relocated 2.5 million people from the overcrowded inner islands to the large, less populated islands of Sumatra and Sulawesi, and latterly to the undeveloped regions of Kalimantan and Irian Jaya. With a population density of around 700 people per km$^2$ on Java, it was claimed that this would offer the landless poor the chance of improved living standards and their own land.

The reality however, as experienced by thousands of resettled families, is that the landless poor of Java have been translocated to a destitute life in the outer regions. Offered between 2 and 5 ha of land along with the seeds, tools and chemicals to grow rice, their relocation has frequently been to remote land, where there is a lack of basic facilities like water and power. Further, the land is often forested due to the lack of available agricultural land; this means it must be cleared, that it is poor quality for growing crops and that it will be quickly exhausted.

The Government acknowledged that it did not have the capacity to resettle such large numbers of people[3] and at least 2000 families, unable to survive under the new conditions, returned home to Java during the economic plan of the early 1980s. Many more people have stayed, reduced to penury. Some 40,000 families have been supported by UN food aid worth US$40 million since 1988[4] but the harsh conditions of life as a transmigrant are most tellingly acknowledged in their higher than average death rates and reduced life expectancy[5].

*Development of Plantations*

Since 1984, in a major shift of transmigration policy, rather than giving out land for self-sufficient food production, the Government has been viewing transmigration as a resource for development and stipulating that resettlement should entail cash crop production as part of a plantation estate.

In January 1992, it was announced that cocoa was one of the three main crops along with oil palm and coconuts to be produced by 42 newly licensed nucleus estate plantation companies and that 500 families had already been moved to support the development of the first 150,000 ha of land, out of a total 750,000 ha allotted to the projects[6].

Linking the transmigration programme with state-run or privately-owned plantation companies, the nucleus estate programme operates by giving smallholders plots of land to grow cash crops around the nucleus of privately-owned land and provides work for them on the central plantation. Transmigrants and the displaced local farmers would benefit through contributing their crop to the centrally-owned operation and receiving work on the central estate. The effects however, have displayed the limitations and short-sightedness of the scheme, as smallholders have witnessed a dramatic fall in their standard of living, sites are being deserted and people are demanding their original land back[7].

The farmers on one coconut estate, funded by the World Bank, sought for the land to be returned to its original status as a self-sustaining community growing a variety of crops from bananas and maize to cloves. The promised US$1000 a year income as a smallholder on the nucleus estate had materialised at as little as US$5, with the company demanding cash repayment for fertilizer, transport and the bank loan for the project. On protesting about their low income, the advice given to these farmers was to plant cocoa[8].

Debt-bound to the company for their land (for which they must pay when their trees come into fruit), dependent upon the crop to ensure income and dependent upon the company to buy it at a fixed price, the effect of cash crop transmigration has been to turn settlers into cheap plantation labour. The broader effect has been the creation of a community which is wholly dependent upon the world market for cocoa and macro-economics.

*The Threat to Diversity*

Since 1986, Irian Jaya, the largely untouched province of West Papua has also been targeted as a location for transmigration and plantation operations. Encouraging foreign capital with tax holidays and the ability to own land, foreign companies including the British Commonwealth Development Corporation as the major backer of a cocoa plantation[9] have already invested in the region. Home to many thousands of tribal peoples, the arrival of transmigration in Irian Jaya has spelled disaster, both for the rainforest and the indigenous people. So far 100,000 settlers have been moved to Irian Jaya; the government's original target of 1 million people would result in the indigenous people (who number only 800,000), becoming a minority in their own land[10].

The transmigration programme, described by *The Ecologist* magazine[11] as the biggest colonisation programme in history, has been condemned globally as an environmental disaster and a denial of human rights for the indigenous peoples involved. Siberut, an island lying off the coast of West Sumatra demonstrates this vividly.

An area of rainforest, home to the indigenous Mentawai peoples has been delineated for a transmigration plantation project to produce oil palm. The area was designated a Biosphere Reserve by UNESCO in 1981, because of its rich, unique ecosystem with a wealth of endemic species. Living in a culture over 3000 years old, the Mentawi live in a harmonious relationship with the environment, farming with co-operation rather than domination through sustainable forms of agriculture.

Destruction of the land erodes genetic diversity and also destroys cultural diversity as the indigenous peoples are unable to maintain their traditional lifestyle and spirituality, and are themselves threatened. This is imminently so on Siberut where 250,000 hectares of rainforest, one-half of the island's area, has been assigned to oil palm plantation and the transmigration of 40,000 people is proposed to work it. Furthermore, the intention is that 2000 of the transmigrants will be single men "for the purpose of assimilating with the Mentawai women".

The fate of the Mentawai women and the future of the people is therein determined[12]. While effectively giving away their land for economic development, the Government's aim is to assimilate tribal peoples throughout Indonesia and to transform them into settled farmers and cultivators[13].

The environmental cost of such development is now visible on a mass scale. Transmigration, including the clearance for cash crop schemes, caused on average one-quarter million hectares of deforestation annually in the mid-1980s (5 times the amount of forest cut for logging)[14]. Although rainforest clearance for transmigration was banned by the President in 1979, the recent economic plan of 1984-89 sited 80% of all transmigration sites in primary rainforest regions[15]. Since 1950, 39 million ha of rainforest throughout Indonesia has been lost[16].

**Chocolate Unwrapped** The Politics of Pleasure

Export earnings from products like cocoa (which increased 5-fold in the 1980s to US$50 million in 1989, despite the fall in price) demonstrate the immediate short-term financial benefit of development, but both the land and the cultural heritage in regions considered resource-rich and under-exploited, are threatened by destruction. Fuelled by the drive to develop, integration of southern nations into the current global cash economy is demanding a high price in the unquenchable exploitation of people and resources.

**Figure 2.** TOP DESTINATIONS OF COCOA BEANS AND COCOA BUTTER IN 1989/90 FROM THE TOP FOUR PRODUCERS [IN TONNES].

**Destination of Ivorian Coast cocoa beans**

| | |
|---|---|
| Netherlands | 258,150 |
| W. Germany | 111,707 |
| US | 95,146 |
| USSR | 55,945 |
| France | 24,971 |
| [UK | 17,829] |

**Destination of Ivorian Coast cocoa butter**

| | |
|---|---|
| France | 8,838 |
| Netherlands | 8,286 |
| UK | 7,392 |
| US | 5,194 |

**Destination of Brazilian cocoa beans**

| | |
|---|---|
| US | 43,135 |
| USSR | 24,800 |
| Netherlands | 8,015 |
| Poland | 7,015 |
| Spain | 6,710 |
| [UK | 3,060] |

**Destination of Brazilian cocoa butter**

| | |
|---|---|
| US | 22,366 |
| Netherlands | 6,457 |
| USSR | 4,910 |
| Japan | 4,097 |
| Argentina | 1,068 |
| [UK | 100] |

**Destination of Ghanaian cocoa beans**

| | |
|---|---|
| UK | 67,020 |
| Japan | 33,200 |
| USSR | 32,800 |
| US | 24,850 |
| W. Germany | 15,580 |

**Destination of Ghanaian cocoa butter**

| | |
|---|---|
| UK | 4,225 |
| Netherlands | 2,800 |
| W. Germany | 300 |

**Destination of Malaysian Cocoa beans**

| | |
|---|---|
| Singapore | 70,742 |
| W. Germany | 28,263 |
| Netherlands | 22,373 |
| US | 15,972 |
| UK | 13,948 |

**Destination of Malaysian cocoa butter**

| | |
|---|---|
| US | 10,527 |
| Netherlands | 5,988 |
| UK | 3,474 |
| Australia | 2,154 |
| France | 1,218 |

*Source ICCO XVII no4 Sept 1991*

# Map Flow of Resources

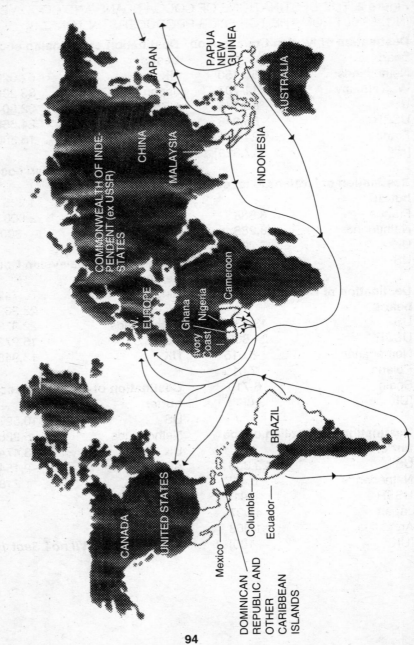

# Pesticides

Since plants were first grown for food, chemicals have been used to preserve crops from the pests competing for the same harvest. As agriculture has become more sophisticated, so have these chemical tools. The use of modern pesticides has played an important part in the dramatic increase in agricultural productivity over the last few decades. From sulphur used by the Greeks and arsenic used in the US from the 1800s, the use of today's deadly array of synthetic organic chemicals is now global and ubiquitous and worth around £15 billion in sales revenue in 1990.

Early modern synthetic pesticides were derived, not through research to promote agriculture, but directly from research into agents useful in war. Developed during World War II, organochlorines like DDT were formulatedto protect soldiers from malaria in the tropical wetlands; organophosphate insecticides such as parathion were designed as nerve gases, and phenoxyacetic herbicides such as 2,4-D were designed to clear vegetation, widely demonstrated later in Vietnam. More recently, other groups of pesticides like synthetic pyrethrins have been developed in response to problems of resistance and resurgence of the pests earlier chemicals were aiming to eradicate.

Utilized for their toxic properties, pesticides are used to kill what are perceived to be threats to the crop. These include, insects, weeds and fungi. Contact with these toxic chemicals however, extends beyond this working remit, and it is this which gives cause for concern as they adversely affect both the health of people spraying them and the surrounding ecosystem. Individuals are exposed involuntarily to pesticide residues through contamination of our food, but exposure to the people who spray these chemicals is more direct. If health and safety practices are adhered to such contact is not necessarily hazardous, but in regions where conditions and safety practices are poor and application is prolonged, especially in the South, workers are continually exposed to the risk of adverse health effects from using these toxic substances.

The acute health effects from using pesticides are increasingly recognised to be widespread. These vary in type and severity depending upon which chemicals are being used. Whilst exact figures are difficult to establish with the paucity of research data, a recent study estimates that pesticides are currently poisoning some 25 million Third World agricultural workers each year. The World Health Organisation estimates that there are 20,000 fatal cases of poisoning by agrochemicals each year worldwide[1]. Most agricultural poisonings occur in the South where cash crop agriculture is expanding and where working conditions are poor, and where pesticide application can be a daily job.

Long term exposure to certain pesticides may result in chronic health effects. Different pesticides pose different types and degrees of such health risks for the workers in contact with such chemicals. Chronic health effects of pesticides however, are much more difficult to gauge and figures are difficult to establish. For example, some organochlorines, such as lindane, aldrin, and dieldrin are believed to be carcinogenic. Lindane has been classified by the EPA as a probable human carcinogen and has also been shown to affect the human nervous system[2].

The chronic effects incurred as a result of pesticide spraying may not show up for months or years until cancer or chronic dysfunction appears when, of course, prevention is too late. World Health Organisation evidence suggests that 37,000 cases of cancer occur annually as a result of pesticide exposure[3]. While her daily work brings a threat to the worker's own health, her unborn children may also be at risk from those agrochemicals that are teratogenic or embryotoxic[4] (see Appendix 1).

Pesticides are also detrimental to the environment as they kill not only target organisms but also affect the wider ecosystem as Rachel Carson so poignantly described in *Silent Spring* (see Chapter 5). Today companies are producing chemicals which are less toxic and environmentally persistent than DDT, yet pesticides by their nature are not ecologically benign and adverse environmental effects are inescapable. In regions of the South especially, where cash crop production is expanding, there is little investigation or analysis of the effect of mass pesticide use.

*Monoculture*

Plantations are constructed agricultural landscapes where row upon row of identical plants or trees cover the land in regular patterns. Such an environment is a landscape of uniformity, one plant dominating to the designed exclusion of all others. This is monoculture. Most cash crops are grown in this way, on vast swathes of land around the world. If you use a natural product for food, clothing or, increasingly, paper and similar products, then it is probably grown in this way.

This concentrated mass production has assisted the huge increase in output and consumption of these products over the last 50 years. As demonstrated in Malaysia, Brazil and Ghana, however, this rush to escalate production has not been in the best interests of all. Nor has it been in the best interest of the earth.

Clearing vast tracts of land to construct cash crop plantations has required the use of increasing amounts of agrochemicals to prevent insects and disease from raging through the single plant crop, made vulnerable to the cycles of the natural world by its monocultural habitat. The monoculture has replaced the rich web of interconnected plants, animals, lifecycles and chains of biological experience. The diverse tapestry of plants and animals in a natural ecosystem has been reduced to those essential to crop production. Such development has destroyed natural ecosystems like the tropical rainforests of Asia and the Americas and has contributed to the concomitant rapid extinction of species. The very future of wild cocoa in the Amazon is threatened by this constant 'development'[5].

Mass monocultural agriculture is also steadily depleting the soil that nourishes and supports it. Nutrients, drawn from the soil in the growth process, are picked, removed and exported as the crop. Without replenishment from the detritus and biomass that accrues as other natural vegetation dies, the soil gradually becomes infertile.

Although cocoa exhausts the soil less than some annual cropping plants, continued cultivation of this crop gradually depletes the soil, as organic matter and nutrients are lost[6]. Nitrogen fertilisers deemed essential in contemporary agriculture do not offer long-term fertility and extended use is damaging to the soil and to the underground water reserves.

Without the natural cushioning of the thick leaf canopy, rains, especially in the tropical regions, pound down upon the ground. Without the vegetation naturally present on the floor of the forest to hold the soil in place, the water washes out the remaining nutrients, contributing to the long-term reduction in fertility. In some regions, the rain is able to wash away the soil itself, depleting the land and silting up the rivers, streams and marine fishing grounds. The loss of soil from the land is one of the biggest environmental problems facing both developing and developed regions today.

In part responsible for decreasing soil fertility and erosion of the land, these methods of crop production lead to the spraying of tonnes of chemicals onto the land daily. Bahia in Brazil for example used on average six tonnes of active ingredient daily in 1986[7].

Plantations need pesticides. Where the natural ecosystem operates in balance, with potential pests held in check by the variety of species present, a plantation is susceptible to one pest raging through the area, unchecked by any natural enemy. Insecticides quickly become essential to the continued productivity of the plantation for, without natural predators, insects multiply unchecked the next season, requiring increasing quantities of the chemical to be effective. Over several brief lifecycles they adapt to be resistant, thus requiring even greater quantities.

There have been advances in pesticide use, where pesticides are used more sparingly and in combination, and newer ones are employed which are more carefully tailored to the pest in question. However these still do not eliminate resistance and the destruction of beneficial species.

Different crops require different approaches with pesticides: cotton for example relies heavily on insecticides due to its long maturing period which allows insects to multiply. Tree crops such as cocoa further require herbicide input to keep the base of the tree free of weeds, and susceptibility to fungal infection also necessitates fungicide.

*Pesticides Used on Cocoa*

At least 30 pesticides are known to be used on cocoa including several members of the Pesticide Action Network's 'Dirty Dozen' (see Figure 3.1). Considered a cheap means of mass control of pests and weeds, agrochemicals have been increasingly promoted in Ghana during the last ten years and are considered an essential element of cocoa production on the plantations of Malaysia and Brazil where cocktails which include some of the most toxic pesticides are applied regularly.

Cocoa, like all crops grown on plantations, is susceptible to an array of diseases, from the witches' broom disease in Brazil (where a fungus causes the branches and pods to dry up and shrivel), to the ubiquitous black pod disease caused by a fungus that attacks the cocoa beans causing them to rot and turn black, estimated to account for the loss of 10-30% of the world crop[8].

Cocoa trees are also threatened by 1,500 species of insects worldwide which are known to feed on cocoa. Only a handful of these, however, do enough damage to the crop to ensure that protective measures are taken against them. Although the use of agrochemicals has increased, little research has been carried out in situ on the adverse health and environmental effects of their use. In Ghana the Cocobod is now taking initial steps to investigate the

environmental effects of the testing and use of pesticides in the cocoa growing regions.

*Malaysia*

In Malaysia women make up around 80% of the 8000 spraying workforce[9].
They dilute and mix chemicals and carry containers full of pesticides around
the plantation. Sprayers pour the toxic concoction into their backpumps and
spray the plantations on foot. The women rarely wear protective clothing;
leaking spray equipment means constant dripping onto the sprayer's skin,
and the spray mist is ingested. The lack of basic safety information can be
witnessed as the women readily mix pesticides by hand and remove block-
ages from the nozzle by mouth[10].

Training and information alerting sprayers to the safety measures and health
dangers of agrochemicals are rare. Where agrochemicals are labelled, the
instructions are ineffective, with many labels printed in English. Without pic-
tograms, even information in the local language is useless to the illiterate. As
plantation management has failed to provide adequate training for workers,
local campaigners are currently running workshops to educate sprayers on
the health effects of agrochemicals. They are currently collaborating on an
Asia-wide programme to educate women about pesticide use[11].

Interviewing female pesticide sprayers in Malaysia as part of that programme, Vasanthi Arumugam's recent book *Victims Without Voice*[12] has
documented the shocking effects pesticide spraying has had on the health of
50 sprayers. Many women recognise that long-term spraying is dangerous to
their health, but they accept frequent skin irritation and rashes, difficulty in
breathing and irregular menstrual cycles as an aspect of life to be endured,
ignoring the threat of these symptoms. Unable to support their families elsewhere, they cannot afford to do otherwise.

Most agricultural workers in Malaysia are well aware that pesticides are dangerous; accidental pesticide poisoning is common and drinking pesticides is
the primary mode of suicide in Malaysia, with 1158 such deaths between
1986 and 1990[13]. Though aware of general health risks, the Malaysian
women interviewed were predominantly ignorant of the initial symptoms of
poisoning such as headaches, tiredness or dizziness caused by the chemi-

cals. Women complained of skin rashes and sought creams to cure them, but less than half recognised that pesticides can enter the body through the skin. The women who sprayed paraquat complained of skin rashes, sore red eyes and discoloured nails (see Figure 3.3). All the women who sprayed carbaryl complained of tiredness and dizziness and all the women spraying dimethoate complained of nausea and tiredness. Half the women spraying lindane complained of skin rashes, with one in five having nausea, difficulties breathing, stomach pain and dizziness. (see Figure 3.2).

*Paraquat*
Described by a plantation field worker as the Sime Derby cocktail, paraquat is a herbicide used voraciously on the cocoa plantations to kill the lush weeds which thrive in the tropical semi-shade. As an inexpensive and widely available pesticide, paraquat is used on most of the plantations in Malaysia as a cheap form of weed control; it isquicker and cheaper to spray than to cut the weeds by hand.

Yet it has been responsible for more human poisonings than any other weed killer, accounting for over a quarter of all poisoning cases in Malaysia in the last decade[14]. Once it is in the body there is no antidote and less than a teaspoonful of concentrated paraquat is lethal when swallowed. Rashes, skin burn and irritated eyes are the common symptoms of poisoning, but these precede the permanent deterioration in the health of the women who mix, carry and spray this weed killer every day. The US safety recommendations for paraquat use suggest full protective clothing at all times, including a rubber suit, rubber gloves, latex goggles and a respirator, yet on a Malaysian plantation less than one in three women are given a pair of gloves[15].

Considered to be a highly dangerous pesticide because of its acute toxicity, paraquat is a member of the Pesticide Action Network's 'Dirty Dozen' (see Figure 3.1) and has been targeted by worldwide campaigns for a global ban. Germany withdrew it in 1983, believing it to be an environmental pollutant, yet the manufacturers, ICI, have appealed and the case is still before court. It was first produced in 1963, and although its patent has now expired, ICI still take around 90% of the market and have a formulation plant in Malaysia[16].

Sahabat Alam Malaysia, the national Friends of the Earth group have been campaigning for a total ban on paraquat in Malaysia since 1985. Yet, whilst the Malaysian Health Minister in 1988 advised plantation managers to pay more attention to workers' health and to encourage safety education and safer practices, the Ministry of Agriculture has no intention of banning the "cheapest and most effective" weed killer on the market[17].

*Pesticides in Brazil*
The position is no better in Brazil. Between 1983 and 1987, 1,384 people suffering from the effects of agrochemicals were seen at Anti-Poison, a health clinic in Bahia, the cocoa growing region of Brazil[18]. This official statistic is a huge underestimate of the problem faced by the agricultural workers using pesticides on the Brazilian cocoa plantations, with many cases going unreported. Brazil is a mass consumer of pesticides, spending over £2 million on British chemicals alone in 1987[19].

Like Malaysia, most of its cocoa crop is grown on plantations and entails a great dependence on agrochemical input. Paraquat is applied along with a range of insecticides including endosulfan and malathion and fungicides like mancozeb and copper compounds, used to reduce fungal infections that cause diseases like witches' broom.

All the major chemical companies sell pesticides in Brazil, many of which are restricted and banned elsewhere and the majority of them are available over the counter in the local shop[20]. CEPLAC, the Government-run cocoa board, is involved in agrochemical research, testing and promotion and provides a long list of chemicals recommended for use, including the more toxic pesticides such as parathion. The smaller producers who often cannot afford the pesticides operate pesticide-free practices using natural fertiliser to feed the soil, pruning to keep down the pests and shade to control weeds, but CEPLAC has been advocating and promoting agrochemical production methods which favour the larger producers. With a continuing commitment to increasing plantation production, Brazil is likely to use increasing quantities of pesticides in future cocoa cultivation[21].

*Ghana*

Under the same increasing pressure to grow cocoa on larger plantations, the cocoa growers in Ghana have been encouraged over the last decade to use more pesticides on their crop. Ghanaian farmers first used chemicals such as nicotine on their crops and then in the late 1950s changed to the synthetics like DDT and lindane. Under the jurisdiction of the Cocobod, they converted to the new-found synthetic insecticides when they found lindane increased the crop production by over 20% in the first four years of use[22]. this saved the amount they could normally expect to lose to the biggest cocoa pest in West Africa, the mirid.

Since the development of cocoa as a crop, the Cocobod has advocated good agricultural practices and controlled and moderated the use of pesticides. As the sole point of distribution for all agrochemicals, they have tested and approved all agrochemicals used; they have controlled quantities used by the farmers by cross-checking the farmers' agrochemical orders with the farm size; and they controlled application by employing, training and equipping sprayers to go out and spray the farms. The Cocobod has approved only two insecticides for use - lindane and propoxur - and is now screening several copper-based fungicides for their efficacy against black pod disease.

Ten years ago, the Ghanaian government requested financial loans from the World Bank and, in exchange, agreed to improve technology including machinery and more chemicals in a push towards privatisation and mass production. As a result, the control of the Cocobod has been eroded and the use of pesticides has been encouraged. Pesticides have become readily available, herbicides have been introduced and the influence of the agrochemical companies has grown. Yet, at the World Bank's insistence, over 20,000 sprayers have lost their jobs, leaving it to the farmers to spray their own crops, without guidance or assistance[23].

Mirids attack the cocoa plants by sucking the sap from the stems and feeding on the cocoa pods and inadvertently creating access for infectious fungi. To the West African farmer, the new-found synthetic organochlorine insecticides that annihilated them with such phenomenal initial results were a welcome revolutionary development. But the miraculous results didn't last, as lindane-resistant mirids emerged after a couple of years and, uninhibited by further spraying, continued to feed on the cocoa crop. Other insects increased in numbers as the chemical altered the ecological balance. The chemicals have promoted previously unknown threats to the cocoa crop from insects such as cocoa pod borers, which are widespread in South East Asia but are now a new problem for the farmers of Ghana.

In an attempt to reduce insect resistance to lindane, the Cocobod approved a second insecticide, propoxur, a carbamate chemical made by Bayer to be used alternatively with lindane in different regions of the country. Although the pests have been contained, the phenomenal results of the early years haven't recurred. Without instruction in spraying and safety and without subsidy, many farmers in Ghana today are no longer spraying pesticides but are using traditional methods and more appropriate technologies, keeping the land clear of rotting matter to reduce the incidence of black pod, using correct shading and manual weeding to keep down the weeds and pruning to protect against pests.

While chemicals are still generally promoted as a cost-effective method of cocoa production in plantation agriculture, the argument about economic progress is even less persuasive when lindane is recognised to be dangerous to human health and an environmental contaminant. After years of testing chemicals on the land for suitability on the crop, the Cocobod is only now beginning to implement a programme of soil analysis to investigate the environmental effects of such agrochemical use[24].

*Lindane*

Whilst cocoa can be grown in Ghana without the mass agrochemical input used elsewhere, pesticides are considered indispensable on plantations. The Malaysian plantation operators consider that there is no alternative to lindane on cocoa; the plantation crop is not viable without insecticides. A 120 hectare (300 acre) site will be sprayed with 15-20 lb of lindane each day respraying each area every two weeks, at a cost of US$1 a hectare (US$2.50 an acre). Twelve people each day would be spraying an area this size with poor equipment.

Lindane is a member of the highly toxic group of chemicals called organochlorines that affect insects by interfering with transmission of nerve impulses. They affect humans similarly. A spoonful will kill a person but smaller doses cause effects ranging from convulsions to vomiting, dizziness and fearfulness as the chemical affects the central nervous system. Even with protective equipment, sprayers in Ghana have suffered skin problems[25]. Chronic poisoning over a time will cause kidney and liver damage (see Appendix 1).

The US Environmental Protection Agency has classed lindane as a probable carcinogen and has restricted its use in the US and it is banned in a further 8 countries, although still approved in the UK (see Figure 3.4). As an environmental contaminant, lindane is very persistent. It is carried vast distances in the air, pollutes surface and ground water and is very toxic to fish. Villagers in Lake Volta in Ghana, unaware of pesticide safety and lindane's potent toxicity, became ill when they poured quantities of it into a lake to fish, eating the dead catch that rose to the surface[26].

Whilst the World Bank has been promoting agrochemical methods of cocoa production in Ghana, lindane, along with paraquat, has been internally reviewed. In response to pressure from environmental groups, the World Bank began to review its pesticides policy in the mid-1980s, publishing a paper in 1985. Criticised by the industry for presenting a 'black list' of agrochemicals, it was sent for redrafting, and reappeared in 1988 for consideration. It recommended withdrawing paraquat and lindane from World Bank funded projects. This recommendation, however, has yet to be implemented, and the organisation has elected to establish committees of investigation; one to look into alternatives to lindane, and the other to investigate the economic implications of withdrawing paraquat from projects.

*Dangers in Production*

Although the more toxic pesticides may be hazardous to use, they are also highly polluting when being made. Toxic chemical production is one of the most environmentally polluting manufacturing practices operating today and many companies have been attacked by the environmental lobby for contaminating the environment with dangerous pollutants and chemical waste.

Inquinosa in Spain has been the focus of a sustained clean-up campaign by Greenpeace over their lindane production, where every tonne of lindane produces 5 tonnes of waste BHC, which is used as an insecticide in its own right but has been rejected by 28 countries as too toxic. It is further contaminated with dioxin, one of the most toxic chemicals known and considered to be the second deadliest substance on earth after plutonium. Since 1976, an average of 30 tonnes of this waste has been put in PVC containers and dumped in the local area around Huesca every day. Lindane from Spain has been exported world wide including to Argentina, Mexico and Brazil[27].

Greenpeace won their campaign in 1989 with the shutting of the plant, yet lindane continues to be made in France by Rhone Poulenc and made the news headlines in 1989 when a tanker carrying five tonnes of the chemical to Indonesia sank in the English Channel, raising fears of major marine contamination, and reminding the public of the threat from chemical pollution[28].

*The Pesticide Trade*

The pesticide trade is growing. In 1985, three million tonnes of pesticides were produced, double that of 1970. Increase in pesticide use has slowed in the North as the market is saturated, but while cash crop consumption continues to rise, use of pesticides - old, new and banned - continues to increase annually in the regions of the South[29]. Trade in pesticides reached US$22 billion by 1990, with 20 corporations controlling 94% of the world market, all of them based in the industrialised nations of the US, Europe and Japan[30].

Sales in the North may further shrink as a result of environmental awareness and increased organic farming, so the chemical companies are looking elsewhere for profits and are expanding new agrochemical markets in the South. By 1991 Latin America, Asia and Africa were using 27% of the world's production of pesticides[31], encouraged by the promotion of cash crop production and pesticide use is expected to further double in the South over the next decade[32].

As public awareness over the effects of chemicals upon our health and the environment grows in the North, pesticide legislation is tightening and pesticides demonstrated as serious threats to the environment and human health are being restricted or banned. One effect, however, has been the increased sales of these chemicals in regions where governments lack the resources, expertise and information for effective pesticide control. The US took ten years to ban DDT after Rachel Carson published *Silent Spring* in 1962, but India, which has been manufacturing it, only banned the import and agricultural use of this chemical in 1990[33].

The majority of the hazardous agrochemicals - identified by the Pesticide Action Network as their 'Dirty Dozen' (see Figure 3.1) - are now restricted to some degree in the North. Yet, many are still known to be used on cocoa on the plantations of Malaysia and Brazil[34].

The UN Food and Agriculture Organisation's Code of Conduct on international use and distribution of pesticides was adopted in 1985 with the aim of reducing the health and environmental hazards. In an attempt to control the trade in hazardous pesticides that are banned or restricted in other countries, a scheme designed to give buying countries information about hazardous pesticides, known as Prior Informed Consent (PIC) was adopted by the FAO Code in 1989 and alerts buying nations to the known health and environmental effects of designated chemicals before they import them[35].

Compliance with the scheme is now mandatory within the EC, and with the support of the industry, it may help to alleviate the current predicament whereby many countries are still using highly toxic pesticides which are banned and severely restricted elsewhere[36]. Whilst PIC is an important precedent, controlling the trade of especially dangerous chemicals will not resolve the hazards of daily chemical use on the health of the ill-equipped sprayers and the adverse effects on the environment.

Chemical intensive cocoa production has certainly facilitated increased production - but to what end and at what cost? Undoubtedly, the plantations of Malaysia are more productive than the smallholdings of Ghana. Yet the quality of the Malaysian bean is considered inferior by the purchasers who consider the Ghanaian bean produced on the smallholdings in West Africa to be the best quality available in the world.

Currently without the financial returns from the crop, the farmers in Ghana are increasingly unable to afford pesticides and are increasingly growing cocoa without chemicals as they revert, out of necessity to traditional forms of agriculture. Whilst pesticides have aided the increase in production, today all producers are getting little return for the crop.

In terms of the risks to the health of the workers who are involved in pesticide application on plantations, the intensive agrochemical method used on cocoa plantations carries a high price. New chemicals are being developed which are less toxic than the older ones, but it is clear that such methods of production are unhealthy and unsustainable. As the trend towards chemical intensive methods of production is encouraged, there is a vital need to consider safe and sustainable methods of production which are not wholly dependent on pesticides.

While cocoa is produced under such conditions, the residues present in our chocolate bars serve to remind us of the hazards of spraying cocoa beans with chemicals and connect our experience as consumers with the experience of the women who are involved in its production.

**Figure 3** PESTICIDES

## 3.1 PESTICIDE ACTION NETWORK'S 'DIRTY DOZEN'

| | |
|---|---|
| Aldicarb | EDB |
| Heptachlor | Camphechlor |
| Lindane\HCH | Chlordane |
| Paraquat | Chlordimeform |
| DBCP | Parathion-ethyl/Parathion-methyl |
| DDT | "The Drins" Aldrin, Dieldrin & Endrin |
| Pentachlorophenol | 2,4,5-T |

*Source: Pesticide Action Network*

## 3.2 INCIDENCE OF SYMPTOMS OF AND COMPLAINTS BY WORKERS SPRAYING LINDANE, AN ORGANOCHLORINE

| Symptom/complaint | % respondents with occasional symptoms | % respondents suffering symptoms very often |
|---|---|---|
| Dizziness | 50 | 30 |
| Nausea | 60 | 20 |
| Stomach Pain | 60 | 20 |
| Vomiting | 20 | 10 |
| Weakness | 80 | 20 |
| Skin irritation/rash | 50 | 50 |
| Difficulty breathing | 30 | 20 |

*Source: Victims Without Voice, Vasanthi Arumugam; Tenaganita & Pesticide Action Network Asia & Pacific, Malaysia 1992.*

**3.3** INCIDENCE OF SYMPTOMS OF AND COMPLAINTS BY WORKERS SPRAYING PARAQUAT, A DIPYRIDYL

| Symptom/complaint | % respondents with occasional symptoms | % respondents suffering symptoms very often |
|---|---|---|
| Nose bleeds | 2 | 2 |
| Cough | 8 | 10 |
| Vomiting | 14 | 8 |
| Generalised muscleache | 8 | 10 |
| Sore red eyes | 18 | 40 |
| Skin rash | 10 | 90 |
| Discoloured irregular nails | 20 | 40 |

Source: Victims Without Voice, Vasanthi Arumugam; Tenaganita & Pesticide Action Network Asia & Pacific, Malaysia 1992.

**3.4** LINDANE RESTRICTIONS AROUND THE WORLD

Countries in which lindane completely prohibited:

| | | | |
|---|---|---|---|
| Belize | Ecuador | Hungary | Japan |
| Netherlands | Singapore | | |

Countries in which lindane is severely restricted:

| | | | | |
|---|---|---|---|---|
| Argentina | Israel | Bulgaria | Mexico | Belgium |
| New Zealand | Canada | Philippines | China | Poland |
| Colombia | Russia | Cyprus USA | Germany | Venezuela |
| Dominica | Yugoslavia | Finland | | |

Source: Consolidated List of Products Whose Consumption and/or Sale have been Banned, Withdrawn, Severely Restricted or Not Approved by Governments, Third Issue UNEP.

# Profit

Most of the cocoa grown today is consumed as chocolate by people in Europe and North America, in a pattern established since the early days of colonial trading which brought the raw materials from the colonised world to be processed and consumed in the industrial nations. According to figures from ICCO[1], the International Cocoa Organisation, 1990/91 was a record year, continuing the trend of the last decade, to surpass two and a half million tonnes of beans produced.

Trade in cocoa, which reached US$4.5 billion in 1987, is conducted mainly between developing countries and the industrialised North[2]. The USA, Netherlands, Germany and the UK alone imported nearly 60% of the world's cocoa beans in 1990[3], in a flow of resources which currently offers precious few benefits to the producers (see Table 8).

Surpassing the need to meet advertising-led consumer demand, the rush to produce more cocoa was generated by rising prices on the commodity markets in the late 1970s. In July 1977, the price reached an all-time high of US 248¢ per lb on the New York market and £3,740 per ton in London[4]. Fired with optimism and excitement, producers planted more cocoa. Yet, whilst Ivory Coast farmers and Malaysian plantation companies turned large areas of land over to cocoa in anticipation of the continued value of the crop, the expected financial returns to the farmers and growers were much reduced by the time the cocoa trees became mature enough to produce fruit. From the 1977 peak, cocoa prices by the end of the 1980s had fallen to less than a quarter of the value, with a pound of cocoa (the harvest of one tree) fetching less than US 50¢.

Cocoa producers have more than met the raw material requirements for the lavish aims of manufacturers to sell more chocolate as bars, drinks or ice creams. While consumption of cocoa has increased throughout the last decade by around 2-3% annually (with record world consumption of over two million tonnes in 1990[5]), this has absorbed less than the huge quantities now produced, leaving massive stocks of around eight months' supply sitting in the warehouses of producers and traders[6]. The supply of cocoa has steadily outstripped demand and the price has tumbled accordingly. Coffee, tea and cocoa all ended the decade with larger stocks in store and all have much lower prices as a result. Indeed, many raw materials mined from the earth or grown as cash crops are worth financially considerably less now than they were at the beginning of the 1980s (see Figure 4).

The fall in price has had a devastating effect on growers, yet at the other end of the cocoa chain, manufacturers with escalating consumption have recorded increasing sales figures and profits. And whilst some traders have gone out of business, others have made big profits in the world's financial centres.

*Commodity Trading*

Commodity trading grew out of the trading companies established in the 17th and 18th centuries to import raw materials back from the colonies. A far cry from that time when street stalls bearing samples of rich and exotic goods were set up in the City of London, trading has become a highly sophisticated practice and has increasingly concentrated into a small number of powerful trading companies who deal with a whole range of commodities.

Since the early 1980s over three-quarters of all the world trading in most food, beverage and agricultural raw materials has been carried out by between three to six companies[7]. In the cocoa trade today, only a few companies predominate, in particular Cargill, Sucres et Denrees and the British based E D & F Mann.

The supply of raw materials has always been subject to a variety of factors from politics to the weather, influencing the price from month to month and year to year. Sometimes based as much on rumour as reality, the price may even vary precariously from day to day. Cocoa prices are established in the financial centres of London and New York. The price is fixed at a daily rate known as the 'spot' rate and its daily seismographic variation creates income for traders and speculators, but undesirable uncertainty for those involved in production and manufacture (see Table 6). For this reason the futures market developed as a mechanism to give some level of price assurance.

Here, one buys and sells not goods but contracts which determine the price of the commodity for delivery on a date set up to a year and a half in the future. The majority of cocoa transactions on the futures market are never physically delivered but are sold on as the chain of traders hedge their investments. Termed the "casino society" by *US Business Week* magazine[8], more money is made in dealing future contracts than the actual commodity. Not surprisingly, trading companies have invested in futures trading operations.

The huge multi-commodity traders operating as buyers and sellers with financial strength and phenomenal networks of information certainly have the advantage in this marketplace. One of the world's biggest cocoa traders E D & F Mann made history in 1990 by acquiring a credit facility of US$250 million from 23 banks[9]. Furthermore, with extensive information networks collating information on all aspects of production, from the expected yields to the impact of the weather, their information is widely used as an indicator of the cocoa market by speculators and cocoa marketing boards alike.

Such is the value of this information that according to the United Nations Conference on Trade and Development (UNCTAD) "The concordance between observed and estimated values is sufficiently good to support the view that futures prices are directly and strongly affected by Gill and Duffis forecasts"[10]. Gill and Duffis, awarded responsibility for collating and publishing cocoa information by the British government after Ghana's independence in 1956, were acquired by E D & F Mann in 1990.

*Cocoa Agreements*
In an attempt to stabilise the cocoa price, representatives of two of the largest cocoa producing countries - Brazil and the Ivory Coast - first met in 1960 and the ensuing decade of negotiation between them and countries which buy cocoa eventually led to a series of price agreements. These agreements created a stock of cocoa which would be used to buffer the price against highs and lows which would control cocoa production.

The First Agreement was signed in 1972 and established the administering organisation ICCO (International Cocoa Organisation) which now has 40 member countries[11]. ICCO would buy cocoa on the market when the price fell below a threshold and would sell when the price rose above a limit. The agreement was renewed in 1975 but the Third Agreement was severely weakened when the Ivory Coast, the biggest producer, and the US, the biggest consumer, failed to agree over the price range and refused to sign. By 1981 ICCO had used up all the funds available to buy cocoa and was unable to borrow to buy more. The price continued to fall until the Fourth Agreement was reached in 1986 when, with renewed funds, the ICCO buyer was able to purchase more stock. However, by February 1988, ICCO had bought all they could and were unable to chase the cocoa price any further. With prices at their lowest for 14 years, the Fourth Agreement is generally considered to have failed[12].

The weakness of the producers' position was plainly displayed in 1987 when the Ivory Coast, led by president Felix Houphouet-Boigny, an ex-cocoa grower himself, stormed out of Fourth Agreement talks and then refused to sell Ivorian cocoa. As the largest producer in the world, the threat of such a reduction in the world supply should have pushed up the cocoa price, but a year later the price continued to fall. The stockpile was so big that such a huge drop in supply did not halt the price trend.

Holding its crops unsold in storage, the Ivory Coast debt soared the next year and in 1989 the government was finally forced to cut state payments to farmers in half to 200 CFA Francs (less than £1) per kg[13]. Farmers, desperate for cash, were accepting prices below this and, as in other cocoa regions, began switching to other crops[14]. Having lost over US$1 billion on cocoa in the previous four years, and pressurised by the International Monetary Fund (IMF) and World Bank for repayment on their US$14 million debt, the Ivory Coast was finally forced to sell. In the largest single deal conducted by the commodity marketing board, the French trader Sucres et Denrees bought 400,000 tonnes (half the stockpile) for an undisclosed price in January 1989[15] and the US multi-commodity dealer Phillips Brothers bought the rest six months later although withdrew from cocoa trading shortly afterwards.

"There is a lot of profit being made" (in the words of a representative of E D & F Mann) from the anomaly between the prices of cocoa products and beans. "It may be good for manufacturers but it is not healthy for the industry as a whole"[16]. In the face of continued overproduction producers have been unable to influence the price they receive for their crops. Set against pressure for continued export expansion and declining prices received as a result, over the last decade, they have been producing ever greater amounts of cocoa for increasingly diminished returns.

In juxtaposition, the thousands of producers worldwide have been selling to a steadily reducing number of companies, as the Northern-based trading and manufacturing companies have been concentrating and consolidating over the last decade. According to Havelock Brewster, the former head of the commodity division at UNCTAD "When many countries sell to what may be perhaps six or less major buying corporations in the North, one cannot expect a fair price to emerge. It is simply not a fair market"[17]. Indeed, less than a dozen companies now account for around 80% of the world's production of chocolate and cocoa products[18].

*The Processing Industry*
The chocolate industry is a three-stage process, from bean to bar - producing, processing and manufacturing. Buying cocoa beans direct or from international commodity traders, processing companies turn cocoa into semi-manufactured chocolate products, cocoa butter and cocoa powder. Like chocolate manufacturers, cocoa processing companies who sell onto the

manufacturing industry enjoy multi-billion dollar sales. This part of the chocolate chain, as with manufacturers, has been concentrating into powerful companies over the last decade.

The processing of the beans has traditionally been carried out in the North
after the beans arrived in the European ports. Amsterdam has always been
the largest cocoa port and continues to be the gateway for the majority of
cocoa into Europe, consequently many processing companies were established there in the last century. Today, three companies predominate in this
part of the process: Cargill, Cacao Barry and W R Grace[19]. Most processing
facilities operate in Europe and the US, with the producers utilising very little
of what they grow. Africa consumes only around 3% of the cocoa it produces
with the remainder being exported mainly to Europe.

Similarly, Latin America exports most of its cocoa for processing and manufacturing, using only 7% of what it grows and Asia processes and manufactures only around 9%[20]. Much greater profits are accrued from processing
beans into the value added cocoa products rather than from producing the
raw materials. In the year that the Ivory Coast, earned US$7 billion from
exporting 700,000 tonnes of beans, Holland made over US$5 billion in export
sales of cocoa products on the import of just 258,000 tonnes of beans and
50,000 tonnes of butter, cake and liquor[21]. The producers are losing out in
the financial benefits of processing and manufacturing raw materials into
chocolate.

Such colonial trading patterns have been promoted by the protective trade
barriers of Europe and the US, which have been happy to import the raw
materials whilst placing high tax levies on processed products and manufactured chocolate entering the country. The EC has a 3% import tariff on cocoa
beans, but a tariff of 12% on cocoa butter and 15% on cocoa paste[22].

As a result, producers have continued to export raw materials whilst the
Northern-based companies have accrued profits from producing the value
added product. Indeed, cocoa only constitutes 12% of the price of a chocolate bar[23]. And while it is difficult for the producers to break into the Northern
markets, the Northern based processors and manufacturers are now moving
factories and facilities into the producing regions, from where they are both
exporting their products and selling to the local population.

*Concentration of the Manufacturers*

Whilst chocolate products proliferate in the shops and supermarkets (numbering over 1000 brand names), they are produced by a diminishing number of giant corporations (see Appendix 2). Today in the UK, the bar of chocolate is likely to be made by one of three companies and, throughout Europe, by one of five (see Figure 5). If you eat a bar in the US, the likelihood is that it is made by one of two companies. Over the last decade, much of the world's chocolate manufacturing industry has amassed into the hands of just five companies, all of whom are based in the North[24].

These transnational companies have phenomenal influence extending beyond the national boundaries of their head offices and revenues which exceed the GNP's of some of the countries in which they operate. These companies are the dominant forces in the world today through their cultural avalanche of commonly available products, their phenomenal financial strength and through their huge advantage in technological innovation.

Few chocolate manufacturing companies have ever owned any cocoa plantations, however. For companies with quick responses and wanting instant returns, investing in huge areas of land, waiting ten years for a crop of cocoa beans and risking the unpredictable aspects of weather, disease and insects has been an unattractive option, although Hershey recently invested in 900 hectares of Belizian land to set up the largest cocoa plantation in the state[25].

These companies generally influence the crops in other ways. Processing and manufacturing companies buy cocoa on the commodity market as well as direct from producers. According to Paul Elshof at SOMO[26], large companies are increasingly buying direct at the farm gate when it suits them, leaving the smaller companies to buy on the market. Rather than investing in a huge land holding, Hershey has encouraged small farmers to grow cocoa around its core plantation, which the company then buys in directly[27].

Since colonial times, manufacturing companies have been experts on cocoa production and they have influenced production since cash cropping began. Companies today are actively involved in the newly developing cocoa producer countries, particularly in Asia. Nestlé have had a joint venture with FELDA, the Malaysian government land authority, to manufacture powder and cocoa butter since the mid 1980s[28] and also have people advising on local cocoa farm management[29].

Cadbury have been in Malaysia since 1986, working with Sime Derby plantations to improve the beans[30], and both Mars and Hershey have been in Malaysia since the mid 1980s working with the local authorities on cocoa quality[31]. With huge research budgets, the manufacturers are continually developing their technological production expertise. In the next step, companies are investing millions of dollars in biotechnological development to produce cocoa trees more suitable to their needs and alternatives to cocoa which will make the cocoa tree redundant all together.

Like the food industry generally, these few powerful companies produce and sell their products worldwide. Nestlé, Europe's largest confectionery manufacturer with 20% of the European market[32], is also Europe's largest food manufacturer. Their products, ranging from ice cream to noodles, coffee to confectionery, and of course baby milk, constitute a significant proportion of goods in the average supermarket trolley the world over. They generated sales in 1989 of over US$30 billion, of which chocolate and confectionery constituted around 15%[33]. Nestlé is the world's biggest cocoa user and alone buys around 10% of the world's cocoa production[34].

In 1990 US-based Philip Morris bought Jacob Suchard and is now Europe's third largest food company, selling chocolate alongside beer and cigarettes with sales of over US$50 billion[35]. This transaction took the head office of three of the five big chocolate manufacturers to America, where Mars Inc. and Hershey Foods have between them cornered over 70% of the American chocolate market[36].

Mars also sells a varied basket load of products from Uncle Ben's rice to Pedigree Chum, earning around US$12 billion in sales annually. Whilst the products are well known, the corporation, by virtue of its private ownership, need not release any business information and Mars is one of the most secretive of the transnational corporations operating today[37].

UK based Cadbury-Schweppes made pre-tax profits of over a quarter of a billion pounds in 1990 from selling chocolate and fizzy drinks[38]. Cadbury has a third of the UK confectionery market, 10% of the European market and was the sixth most profitable food company in Europe in 1988[39].

**Chocolate Unwrapped** The Politics of Pleasure

The pursuit of profit has taken these companies over national borders and their products across the confectionery displays. The 'liberating' economic policies of the 1980s, which removed tax restrictions for big businesses and encouraged corporate expansion, facilitated the growth of huge companies and transformed them into giant corporations, witnessed by the rate of company mergers and acquisitions which reached record levels over the last decade. This expansion has been well demonstrated by the confectionery companies.

Cadbury have bought up companies throughout Europe and America but have resisted take-over themselves, unlike their rivals of nearly a century, Rowntree, who succumbed to a take-over by Nestlé in 1988[40]. As one of the three companies (along with Mars and Cadbury) (see Table 7), who between them took 80% of the UK market, Rowntree was a big attraction to those companies eager to supply a chunk of the 500,000 tonnes of chocolate eaten annually by the British[41]. In one of the biggest corporate take-overs in UK history, Nestlé received a quarter of the British confectionery market (and the best selling British brand, Kit Kat) and assumed a 20% share of the European confectionery market[42].

*New Markets*

According to market reports, consumers in the North cannot eat much more chocolate than we are consuming now. Western Europe and North America currently account for two-thirds of the two million tonnes of chocolate eaten annually worldwide[43] (see Table 8). But, if the rate of consumption in the established regions slows down, profits and hence the future of the companies are threatened unless they can sell elsewhere. Whilst Americans continue to eat a few more solid chocolate bars and Europeans are finding a little extra space for more filled chocolate products, it is to the Far East and Japan that the companies are eager to sell their products next.

Chocolate is relatively new to Japan. Lacking a traditional sweet diet, the Japanese have been eating chocolate in increasing quantities since the 1960s[44]. All the major companies are keen to enter the Japanese market. Rowntree fixed a deal to sell Kit Kat with the large Japanese corporation Fujiya in 1972[45] and it is now the fifth selling brand in Japan[46]. Nestlé have begun a joint venture with Fujiya to further promote confectionery sales[47]; and Hershey have also been involved in a venture to sell their brands in Japan[48].

The confectionery industry is still dominated by the Japanese and is concentrated into the hands of a few companies, with five companies controlling 70% of the sales[49]. Worth in total over US$6 billion in 1990, annual per capita consumption has doubled in the last ten years, to three-quarters of a kilo a year[50], reflecting marketing ploys such as the imported Valentine's Day in February and the innovative White Day in March when white chocolate is bought and given as gifts.

Japan is not the only region in which companies are eager to sell their products. Having already spent time in producing regions working with producers to ensure supplies of raw materials, all the major companies are eager to sell chocolate in the developing markets of the Asia Pacific region. Not only setting up distribution companies and licensing arrangements, the companies are also establishing manufacturing plants to make the products in situ.

Suchard have established distribution companies and licensees throughout the region[51]. Nestlé, having already established a company in Malaysia in the mid 1980s, is now planning to invest in another factory to produce chocolate products[52]. Mars is building a factory in China to make M & M's, after their sponsorship of the Asian games in Peking in 1990 resulted in soaring sales, regardless of the price (which at US 50¢ is equivalent to a tenth of the average weekly wage)[53].

In order to satisfy the urge to sell more, the transnationals are investing in research into tropical chocolate: chocolate which melts at a higher temperature, in order to sell more in hot climates. The Americans have patented their developments and the Japanese have already achieved this.

As the transnational companies seek to increase sales, the people of the Third World, who are losing out in the commodity marketplace, are being targeted as the next customers and packaged pieces of value-added Western culture are now being produced and sold in these regions.

**Figure 4** COMPARATIVE COMMODITY PRICES 1980 & 1990

| Price* of commodities | 1980 | 1990 |
|---|---|---|
| cocoa | 2602 | 1271 |
| coffee | 3399 | 1965 |
| tea | 2157 | 2039 |
| sugar | 631 | 276 |
| palm oil | 583 | 289 |
| rice | 433 | 286 |

* = in US$ per tonne

*Source: UNCTAD Monthly Commodity Price Bulletin UN, NY.*

**Figure 5** EUROPEAN MARKET BY COMPANY

| European Market Share | % |
|---|---|
| Nestlé | 20 |
| Mars | 16 |
| Suchard | 12 |
| Cadbury Schweppes | 10 |
| Ferrero Rocher | 9 |
| All Others | 33 |

*Source Financial Times 30/9/92*

# *Alternatives*

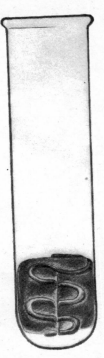

# Biotechnology

Unknown to the majority of consumers, there are now a number of foods available in our supermarkets that have been made or grown as a result of genetic modification in a laboratory. This fact isn't included on labels - and needn't be - and stores do not openly display them as such, yet genetically manipulated 'novel' foods have quietly crept into our shopping whilst the biotechnology debate, that concerning the safety and wisdom of rearranging the basic building blocks of life, continues[1].

Since the 1970s and the first scientific manipulations of genes, biotechnology has been hailed by its proponents as the route to abundance and health and as the solution to the environmental violations of our age. The major focus for development has been the medical and agricultural applications of drugs and tools to cure disease and the manipulation of animals and plants

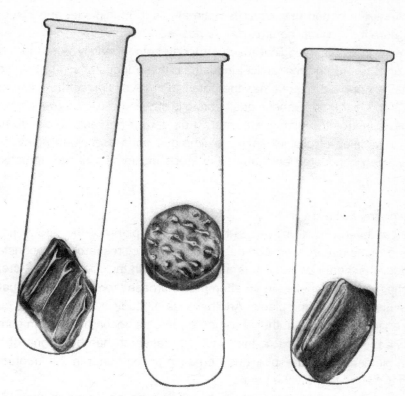

to improve and increase food yields. Alternative voices have raised concerns about the risks of designing and manipulating living material that is then released into the environment as independent self-replicating organisms.

Safety considerations notwithstanding, the value system which sanctions the ownership and manipulation of life for profit has been questioned by a range of concerned individuals. Such an approach does not resolve the fundamental problems of disease, hunger and environmental degradation but camouflages them, offering the hope of miraculous scientific reprieve and detracting from the need to make the radical changes in our values necessary for the world to be a safe place to live.

Without any resolution of these disparate views, biotechnology has emerged over the last twenty years from the laboratories of academia into an expanding multi-million pound business. Its main aim is to manipulate and improve upon nature for primarily commercial purposes.

Investment in biotechnological research today comes mainly from the food, agrochemical and pharmaceutical industries, those industries with the most to gain. This applied science has the potential to revolutionise the origin and production of our food. Genetic engineering is causing cows to produce more milk and constructing plants with more fruit, larger harvests of seeds and greater quantities of oils. Research to improve upon and clone plants has already been conducted on many cash crops including tobacco, tomatoes, bananas and oil palm.

*Improving the Bean*

Cocoa has been and continues to be a favourite plant for the attentions of the gene manipulators who pursue several paths of research in a constant search for the 'better bean'. Some are tinkering with the cocoa genes, creating higher-yielding varieties in an attempt to increase the quantity and quality of beans produced by the plants. Another area of study is the attempt to convert one kind of oil into another, in order to recreate cocoa butter from something cheaper like palm oil. A third mode of research has been one of the biggest biotechnological aspirations - creating cocoa butter in the laboratory without the need to grow the plant.

The largest biotechnological research programme on cocoa in the US is investigating ways to increase the yield of the cocoa plants. In 1986 Pennsylvania State University was endowed with a US$1.5 million research budget to investigate the molecular biology of Theobroma Cacao[2]. Funded by two groups, the American Cocoa Research Institute and the US Chocolate Manufacturers' Association which is supported by 15 companies including Nestlé, Hershey and Mars, this programme is probably also the largest biotechnological research on cocoa worldwide[3].

Aiming to develop and clone high-yielding cocoa plants, researchers are seeking ways to increase the number of pods on each tree, increase the number of beans in each pod and also make larger beans of uniform quality. According to Dr. Paul J. Fritz, head of the research programme, the "cocoa plant takes three to five years to bear fruit, and the industry cannot afford to wait that long"[4].

Such remodelling of living material is well within the bounds of biotechnological capability. By discovering the biological tools required to cut and extract the genetic template for attributes such as 'large numbers of beans in a pod' from a plant that has this feature and to then insert it into a plant together with a gene that displays 'many pods', a plant with 'many pods containing many beans' can be created.

Isolated genes are the materials of the biotechnologist, using enzymes like scissors to cut and paste the molecule of DNA into which is encoded the instructions and inheritance of each cell. Having identified and isolated a coded instruction such a piece of DNA can be encapsulated in a bacteria and kept indefinitely in a freezer. When the characteristic is required it can be inserted into the genetic material of another cell causing the cell to reproduce it and hence the organism to assume the characteristic.

The researchers at the Pennsylvania State project are analysing the genetic make-up or genome of the cocoa plant and building up a library of cloned genes to be used as the vital ingredients for future cocoa genetic engineering. It is by the analysis and mapping of the genetic make-up of the cocoa plant that they hope to make further modifications to the plant. One idea is to make the trees resistant to fungi and viruses that devastate so much of the crop and against which large amounts of fungicides are used regularly.

*Creating In-built Resistance*

The biotechnologists' intention is to adapt plants by adding the genes that will protect them from attack or kill off the pests when they come into contact. Rather than exploit the potential for environmental protection, they are also seeking, by adding a gene conferring chemical resistance, to create a plant that will be resistant to the deadly effects of pesticides, thereby removing the need for caution when spraying the crop area.

These latter kinds of developments have been pursued voraciously by the agrochemical companies who are seeking to build resistance to their own pesticides into a variety of cash crops. The trait for glyphosate resistance, for example, (marketed as *Roundup* by Monsanto), has already been transferred to tomatoes, cotton, tobacco and soybeans[5]. This industry is spending millions of dollars in research to manipulate plants to so that they will be sustained through an onslaught of weed killer. According to Lester Brown of the World Watch Institute in Washington DC "Whilst pest and disease resistance are commonly touted as major goals in corporate crop development programmes, resistance to herbicides which will in fact increase the use of these chemicals - is receiving R&D (research and development) priority"[6].

Some plants made resistant to herbicides by the inclusion of genetic material, are currently being field tested and are expected to be on the market in the mid-1990s when the company will sell the plant together with the pesticide in one package. Already bromoxynil-resistant cotton is on sale in the USA and atrazine-tolerant canola in Canada. All the main chemical corporations are pursuing such research, with rewards worth millions of pounds in both seeds and herbicide sales as the farmers plant seeds that they can spray with the matching pesticide that they know will not affect the crop.

Dow Chemicals have developed 2,4-D-resistant tobacco and Rhone Poulenc have produced resistant carrots. Together with Union Carbide, both are seeking to create other 2,4-D-resistant crops including maize, rice and barley that would promote the increased sale and use of old organochlorine chemicals, widely recognised by environmentalists to be highly toxic and polluting[7]. While some research has focused on creating resistance to newer, less dangerous pesticides, this advanced science is also giving the old, toxic chemicals a new lease of life.

Regardless of engineered pesticide resistance, all engineered plants are dependent upon an increased use of pesticides, because of their genetic vulnerability. Being plants of identical genetic make-up, once a pest is able to attack one plant, it will sweep throughout the whole area of trees or crop, unhindered by the variability and individual character of naturally occurring plants. Requiring greater use of pesticides than a genetically diverse area, this has contributed to increased pesticide use on the plantations of hybrid plants and the environmental threat is predictable as genetic diversity is destroyed.

While biotechnological developments do not bode well for the protection of the earth from pesticide damage, the release of these developments without due consideration to the risks is worrying environmental groups. Release of genetically modified organisms into the environment has already occurred. By March 1990, over 100 open air trials had taken place, including 13 in the UK, at which scientists have released experimental products including bacteria to stop frost and viruses that act as insecticides[8]. Scientists admit that, without further ecological understanding, they cannot predict the full outcome of such releases upon the environment.

Transfer of genes from crops to wild plants is possible if genes jump from one species to another and releases are hard to monitor. A report by the Royal Commission on Environmental Pollution considers that, whilst most releases are not hazardous, some could have serious environmental impact[9]. As such, organisms have the potential to provide abundant harvests of food, but at their worst they may be the pollution of the future - alive and able to reproduce, migrate and mutate.

### Manipulating the Cocoa Plant

The chocolate industry is also attempting to make a cocoa tree, a native of the tropics which has always grown in humid heat and flourished in tropical rainstorms, resistant to cold weather and lack of water. The potential for such genetic manipulation seems limited only by the knowledge of where to find the appropriate command on the genome. If such commands are available they can be spliced in and the cell or organism will act.

The Pennsylvania State project is currently concentrating on increasing the amount of cocoa on the trees and modifying the relationship of the trees to pesticides and the immediate environment, but plans have been revealed to modify what is actually inside the bean itself. One mode of research will attempt to increase the fat content of the beans, a mere 1% increase of which would provide manufacturers with extra cocoa butter currently costing millions of dollars annually.

A further imaginative development would take a gene from an African shrub that produces a supersweet protein called thaumatin and insert it into the cocoa plant resulting in the plant producing sweet cocoa, making chocolate without the need to add sugar. Such projects may seem far-fetched at the present, but according to Dr Fritz "within a few years we could be testing these things experimentally"[10]. Hailed as a dieter's dream by the cocoa researchers, consumers would not be the only ones to benefit from such a big reduction in sugar consumption[11].

Biotechnology is muddying the edges of genetic integrity and the diversity of living organisms through the exchange of genetic material. It is also directed towards producing massive genetic singularity, as biotechnologists seek to clone their work to replicate, disseminate and sell the result. Having perfected a design, industry owns, clones and proliferates genetically identical copies of the new plant. Widespread adoption of genetically engineered plant varieties by farmers is dependent upon the fast mass production of such cloned plants. The technique to produce unlimited numbers of these genetically identical plants in the laboratory at high speed is known as micro propagation and has been attempted arduously with a number of crops. Researchers have yet to succeed with such propagation of cocoa and, whilst some experts are not convinced of the viability of mass production by this method, nor that the method will be proven commercially viable, the head of the Pennsylvanian State project is optimistic that success in this endeavour "could come at any time"[12]. Hershey Foods have already filed a European patent application for a tissue culture method of production of cocoa clones[13].

While there are problems with the micro propagation of cocoa clones, hybrids produced by more traditional means are currently being grown on the plantations of Malaysia and are contributing to a great increase in cocoa yields (and pesticide use) for the plantation companies. Although the massive increases in the national production of cocoa during the 1970s were largely due to large increases in the area growing the crop, the application of science has been responsible for raising yields in the last ten years. Production on the plantations increased both with the prerequisite agrochemical inputs and as hybrid, high-yielding cocoa plants designed to produce more cocoa have been grown commercially.

Compared to the world average of 350-400 lb per acre, the Malaysian cocoa yields have reached a staggering 1200 lb per acre, now trebling the average production[14]. This is already a phenomenal increase in the quantity of beans produced, yet biotechnologists are anticipating that new varieties together with intensive cropping methods will be able to produce up to 3000 lbs per acre[15].

*Effects on Producers*
While the plantation companies have invested in this research and will enjoy the benefits of increased yields, it is unlikely that smallholders will get to see the benefits of better yields from hybrid plants. Without the facilities to invest in the research and the funds to support the hybrids, which are expensive plants and require extensive use of pesticides as a result of their genetic vulnerability, smallholders will be unable to compete.

Ironically, the argument presented by many advocates of biotechnological development is that it will benefit the producers in the Third World by raising yields and increasing income. Yet smallholders are even more likely to lose out as such advanced technologies, requiring chemicals and designed for mass production, are most likely to be used by those with investment power. Without capital, the smallholders are severely disadvantaged in the race for scientifically improved yields.

The effect on the smallholders, currently producing 50% of the world's cocoa, is predictable; such circumstances can only increase the trend towards mass scale plantations, concentrated in the regions of the world where these structures are already in place.

The effect of market economics over the last decade has further demonstrated the effect of massively increasing production, as the price of the majority of commodities on the world markets, and cocoa in particular, has dropped through the floor. The development of high-yielding varieties is likely to lead to overproduction, declining prices and economic instability in cacao-producing countries as advanced technologies and high-yielding varieties facilitate a shift from small scale producers to large scale plantations. The buyers, meanwhile, enjoy the benefits of cheap cocoa.

Although the increasing output has now made Malaysia the fourth largest cocoa producer in the world, the Malaysian cocoa is considered by the manufacturing industry to be of a poor quality. It consequently receives a lower price than the more valuable West African beans and is in less demand. The problem is considered to be the high acidic and low chocolate flavour of the beans, attributed in part to the Malaysian mass production methods. These methods fail to produce high quality cocoa because they do not replicate the drying and fermentation methods of the Ghanaian smallholders who produce the top quality West African beans[16].

Several manufacturers are currently pursuing biotechnological techniques to improve the quality of the cheap, plentiful, plantation-produced Malaysian beans. Cadbury have implemented research and develoment projects to improve the fermentation of the beans and Nestle has a similar project under-way. The Malaysian government, eager to increase sales to the big buyers, has invested in a joint biotechnological research project with Mars to improve the fermentation techniques[17].

*Searching for Substitutes*

Other developments seek an alternative route to genetically engineered food profits. Substitution of cocoa butter is not a new idea in the chocolate indus-try. Manufacturers began using other fats and oils in the 1970s, when the price of cocoa was high, simply replacing some of the cocoa butter content with other cheaper products. However, the amounts that could be used in chocolate manufacture were limited by their taste, which failed to imitate cocoa perfectly, and by legislation clarifying that a product made from such substitutes could not be labelled chocolate.

While the principle of substitution remains the same, biotechnological devel-opments are becoming highly sophisticated, using modified fats and oils from other commodity crops that have been converted to imitate cocoa butter. Several companies have already patented processes that use genetically engineered enzymes which act on another vegetable oil to modify its struc-ture, until it resembles cocoa butter.

Genencor in the US has filed patents on a process to upgrade cheap palm oil into expensive cocoa butter; Fuji Oil Company in Japan has filed a patent to develop cocoa butter substitutes from olive, safflower and palm oil[18]; and some patents even mention whale and fish oils[19]. Unilever currently controls around half of the cocoa butter substitutes market and is one of the biggest manufacturers of edible oils[20]. Other companies in the US are investigating enzyme techniques to convert palm oil into cocoa butter.

These technologies have yet to prove themselves commercially, but experts consider that they will be on the market in the next few years. In doing so, they have the potential to completely alter the edible fats and oils trade, as dependence on expensive products like cocoa butter diminishes and is replaced by cheaper, modified alternatives like palm oil. "New technologies have the potential to overturn oils and fats markets by reducing reliance on high priced imports such as cacao butter. Discontented with the need to import, companies will produce similar oils from domestic sources, in the process even creating oils not found in nature"[21].

Such technology is already affecting the sugar trade, as sugar substitutes can be made from maize and, potentially, from an increasing variety of starch sources from potatoes to artichokes. With the potential for our food to be processed from interchangeable sources of the basic nutritional elements of our diet - fats, starches, oils, proteins - this technological development may completely alter not only the trade in the raw materials which constitute it, but the production of food itself.

Producers will be competing in a global market of molecular commodities. The essentially tropical commodities used in the manufacture of chocolate could come in the future, not just from the tropical South but also from commodities like soybeans and maize, grown in the rich industrialised North. The raw material would be bought not for what it really is, but for what its basic nutritional element can be used to make[22].

*The Redundant Cocoa Tree*

If the endeavours of alternative genetic engineering projects on cocoa are successful, the cocoa tree itself may become redundant. Developments in cell culture, successful with a number of products, have been explored with cocoa. The techniques attempt to make cocoa butter in the laboratory by taking cuttings of the cell tissue that produces the cocoa butter and allowing the cells to proliferate in artificial conditions. Supported by the manufacturing industry, scientists have been actively attempting to produce cocoa butter from cells in a test tube for several years. Hershey foods have funded research at Cornell University to produce cocoa butter using tissue culture, but the technique has yet to be fully successful.

It can be done, but, at US$100 per lb compared to the normal cost of US$4 per lb, it is expensive[23]. If the product could be produced profitably however, the benefits for the manufacturers would extend much further than price; obtaining raw materials would be a faster, efficient and more predictable process. The quality would be uniform, built to match company requirements and the supply would be regular, unaffected by the weather, the seasons, price or politics.

Current opinion, including that of the head of cocoa research at Pennsylvania State, considers it unlikely at the current time that laboratory-produced cocoa butter will become economically viable, but such techniques have been successful for other products, including another important constituent of chocolate - vanilla.

Vanilla is one of the few products successfully created in a lab, with two US companies claiming that they can produce vanilla from plant cell culture. By taking tissue cuttings from the vanilla plant and growing it in solution in the lab, the cells that produce the vanilla flavouring proliferate in the test tube. According to reports in the industrial press[24], it can be produced for around US$25 per lb. This is dramatically cheaper than natural vanilla, which currently costs around US$1200 per lb (synthetic vanilla costs around US$6, but doesn't taste as good). This difference in price represents a huge cut in costs to the food industry which worldwide spends around US$200 million on vanilla flavourings annually.

It remains unknown whether the large scale production of such biovanilla is economically viable, but, with patents pending, there is a good chance it will be marketed before the end of the decade. If a laboratory-produced substance does compete with the real thing, the biggest concern with this technological development is the future of the 100,000 vanilla farmers of Madagascar, Indonesia, Cormoros and Réunion, for whom vanilla, worth annually around US$100 million, is a major crop.

*Implications for the Future*
The assumption that we can patent and own the identity of the crops that

feed us is far removed from the Mayan relationship with the land and with their sacred plants. The rhetoric of the industry about Third World benefits is juxtaposed against the cost of the patented improved versions of the original, natural and freely exploited genetic wealth of the South. Industry argues that their biotechnological developments will assist the Third World producers to improved yields and increased income. The reality for the majority however will be dispossession as cocoa prices fall further through over-production and as they cannot afford higher yielding varieties.

The development of these varieties is likely to lead to greater economic instability, rather than economic wealth. In those regions dependent upon income from this crop, the advanced technologies will promote the shift from small-holders to plantations in developments which support chemical-intensive mass production methods, requiring increased quantities of pesticides. As alternative developments to produce cocoa in the lab would make crop production redundant all together, the cocoa producers of the South have an uncertain future.

Given the potential to radically alter our relationship with the world around us, contemporary biotechnological achievements have reached a pinnacle of a human-centred, mechanistic world view in the drive to control nature. Scientists are applying a set of criteria appropriate to one sector of 20th century Western existence to alter in an instant the global ecological interactions that have evolved over the course of many centuries and which have the potential to endure much longer. Rather than dealing with the fundamental problems of hunger, poverty, and ill health through radical resolution, biotechnology is proposing to side-track us into a bright, designed future where humans can impose instant improvements throughout the biological world based upon a narrow set of unenlightened criteria and short-term vision.

# Conscious Consumption

Lasting solutions to both ecological and development problems are being sought as a result of increased awareness of both environmental and Third World issues. With the recognition that environment and development are crucially interrelated, these perspectives, hitherto considered separately, are becoming incorporated in a holistic view.

Plantation agriculture which requires large quantities of agrochemicals has been widely promoted by governments and the economic institutions who consider it the most cost effective method of crop production. Furthermore, industry and plantation owners have invested in creating genetically modified plants which have very high yields but are further dependent upon chemicals. While output has increased, these methods have resulted in ecologically unsustainable practice; land is degraded, biodiversity is threatened, and production has become dependent upon chemical inputs.

Agrochemical use is expected to double in the South over the next decade as cash crop agriculture expands, yet environmental effects are generally unmonitored, and working in poor conditions, with little information or protection, the adverse health effects on agricultural workers are widespread. Indeed, production has entailed a degrading lifestyle for those who work on plantations, where the production of cheap cocoa has taken precedence over quality of life, the provision of sufficient wages and healthy working conditions.

Western paradigms have spread with the trend towards 'development'. Promoted by Southern governments in the hope of accruing foreign exchange from the export of raw resources, and demanded by world bankers seeking repayment on debt, Third World nations have been encouraged to expand their cash crop economies. Cocoa growers the world over have responded to calls to meet the mediated desire of the North for chocolate. Yet the massive push to cash crop development has caused hardship to vast numbers of people in the cocoa growing regions, as sustainable ways of life have been eroded with the demands to produce crops for export.

Blind to the predictable scenario of indiscriminate global commodity expansion leading to falling prices, cash crop production for export has been promoted heavily by economic insti-

tutions over the last decade in the developing regions. Individual governments and the global economic institutions like the World Bank and IMF
encouraged growers to grow cocoa at a time that the price was high, with a
short term vision and a rationale which failed to predict that the price would
fall as a result of over production.

This policy has facilitated the continued flow of cheap raw resources to the
North, whilst the South has received little benefit. Now, as individuals and
governments have become dependent upon the crop, the price has fallen to
its lowest in two decades, leaving small farmers throughout the regions
unable to feed themselves and now growing their own food, whilst plantation
owners are considering converting their plantations to another commodity in
the hope of remaining profitable, despite the fact that the same scenario may
repeat itself.

For nations such as Ghana which have been placed under tight economic
stricture by the IMF, the results of 'development' have left tens of thousands
of people in poverty, dependent upon income from a cash crop and unable to
provide for themselves. Not able or willing to toil to export a crop for no
return, people are returning to growing food where they can. These current
circumstances highlight the damaging and illusory nature of 'development',
which must be addressed by the North. The shift from a sustainable lifestyle
into a system of expansion and export has left individuals very vulnerable to
the trends of the global economic system, has had ecologically damaging
effects and has stripped people of the means to secure their own livelihood.

*Fair Trade*

Fair trade organisations (established to effect a more equitable trading relationship) promote co-operative rather than competitive trading principles.
They link up with small producers and take care to ensure that the producers
chosen are themselves operating in a fair and democratic manner.

Organisations in Holland have led the way in such alternative trading ventures. Fair trade coffee has been available in Dutch supermarkets for several
years and has taken a 3% share of the market both in Holland and
Switzerland, and is now sold in Belguim and Germany. In Britain, Café
Direct, is now available to consumers.

Fair trading in Holland has been pioneered by the Max Havelaar Foundation, which does not package its own brand but awards its fair trade seal of approval to coffees imported under fair trade terms. The minimum price guaranteed to growers is around three times that given on the world market. In order to avoid dependence on this seal, only a limited part of the exportable produce of each co-operative can be sold under the fair trade conditions. Max Havelaar also encourage co-ops to diversify agricultural production in order to avoid monoculture and the ensuing environmental damage.

After demonstrating their success with coffee, Max Havelaar, along with a consortium of other organisations including British based Twin Trading, has been working to promote fair trade chocolate throughout Europe and plans to launch a range of products in Holland by Autumn 1993. Max Havelaar is currently developing links with cocoa producing co-ops who operate in a democratic manner and at the same time produce a high quality cocoa.

Already, Traidcraft market *Mascao*, a Swiss bar which comes from a co-operative cocoa producing venture in Bolivia[1]. El Ceibo has been producing cocoa since the 1970s. The co-operative developed out of a pioneer settlement in the 1950s which brought people down from the densely populated yet infertile Altiplano highlands of Bolivia to resettle in the lowlands and it grew as the settlers realised they would survive only by working together and supporting each other.

Spread out along the Beni River in the Bolivian lowlands, El Ceibo consists of 36 small co-operative groups numbering around 800 members and their families. Each member cultivates cocoa on one or two hectares of land, bringing their crop to a central processing and marketing post. From the lowlands, the co-op transports the cocoa by truck up through the narrow winding high Andean mountain roads to La Paz from where it is taken along the old silver trading route to the sea for export. Most of their cocoa comes to Europe[2], where it is marketed through fair trade organisations around the EC and offers an alternative to mainstream products. Alternatives such as these are becoming increasingly available, but need the support of consumers.

Most crops produced on small co-operative farms involved in fair trade coffee and cocoa ventures are produced without the need for large chemical inputs by virtue of their labour intensive methods. Some of these farmers are now beginning to recognise the financial value of producing crops without chemicals and are marketing their crops as organic. Around one-third of the cocoa produced by El Ceibo is grown like this, for which the producers receive a premium of around 300% from their fair trade partners. The cocoa can then be used to make organic chocolate. This is more expensive but it more accurately reflects the real cost of chocolate, and presents consumers with an ecologically conscious alternative to mass chemical production.

*Organic*

The use of chemicals on cocoa has been widely advocated for successive decades as the means to ensure greater harvests. Yet the small farmers are now rediscovering through necessity, that cocoa can be successfully grown without intensive pesticide input - by utilising traditional methods of weeding, shading, pruning and clearing away waste. Currently in Ghana, where farmers are struggling to survive the low prices paid for cocoa, the use of chemicals is not widespread because they cannot afford them[3]. With the loss of government subsidies for such inputs, the farmers are reverting to traditional methods of management to reduce the threat from insects and disease.

The use of hazardous pesticides has been constantly criticised by environmentalists and health workers, and now some of those who have hitherto advocated widespread agrochemical use are beginning to reconsider its limitations, as insect resistance is now undermining the efficacy of the chemical intensive approach to cash crop production. Insect resistance is on the rise, in response to which, a holistic view of integrated methods of pest management is emerging. Such techniques take into account the whole ecosystem in order to utilise natural predators and use good farming practices to moderate pest damage.

Despite the early delight of the farmers who saw their crops thrive under a fine mist of chemical spray, natural methods are beginning to be seen to be more economic in some places. The Indonesian government recently successfully banned the use of numerous agrochemicals on rice for economic reasons as too much of the crop was being lost to pests which had become uncontrollable by chemical means[4] and a similar approach can be promoted with many other crops, including cocoa.

As Rachel Carson pointed out at the time of writing *Silent Spring*, around 98% of entomologists were working on chemical methods of control of pests and only 2% looking at biological methods[5]. Although pesticide consumption overall is growing in the South, an altered perspective on the use of agro-chemicals offers the opportunity to lead scientists back to ecological solutions to crop management problems. The World Bank, established to investigate alternatives to lindane may present an opportunity to explore the possibilities of integrated pest management for cocoa under monoculture conditions[6].

However, it is clear that smaller farms, which find it increasingly difficult to survive under current terms of trade, offer an ultimately more sustainable and ecologically viable product. Indeed, it is an ecological irony that the success of the expansion in chemical intensive cocoa farming, which precipitated the fall in the price, has brought in its wake the renewal of chemical free methods of production.

Ethical consumption comes hot on the heels of the green consumerism of the latter part of the 1980s, yet these two enlightened views of our responsibilities as consumers cannot exist in isolation of each other, are interrelated and in fact are derived from the same source. A study carried out by Mintel, *The Green Consumer (1991)*, clearly predicted that ethical consumers, who incorporate an array of concerns for the environment, social justice, economics, people and animals, would become an important force during the 1990s. Any holistic perspective of the foods we buy raises ecological as well as ethical considerations and consideration of the inequities of the current trading system cannot occur in isolation from awareness of the environmental damage caused by the widespread promotion of intensive Western models of agriculture.

Ecologically benign and ethically sound cocoa production is viable and products are now available and should be encouraged as the most favourable consumer option. This is, nevertheless, a consumerist answer to a problem requiring a more fundamental resolution. Comparatively, fair trade initiatives are small and present a limited opportunity for trade based upon sustainable principles. Current developments in the 'New World Order' - the creation of free trade zones in North America and Europe and the Uruguay round of

GATT (General Agreement on Tariffs and Trade) - are rapidly strengthening a trading system which perpetuates impoverishment and environmental degradation. While modifications can improve an unfair and ecologically damaging system, a long term solution must be based upon socially just and ecologically sustainable principles, rather than on market forces and the priority of profit. This requires a radical change in our views on trade, economics and lifestyle.

*Medium-term Strategies*

As a medium-term strategy, countries need to find ways to reduce their dependence upon cash crops. Countries such as Ghana, which are dependent upon one or two commodities, have demonstrated the degree of impoverishment caused by falling prices over the last decade. Reducing economic dependence by crop diversification provides a buffer against the vulnerability created by the vagaries of the commodity markets.

Economic institutions have been focal in the policies encouraging countries to expand one crop, yet many would be in a much better position to determine their own economic destiny if the burden of debt were alleviated. Producers could improve their income from raw resources by developing their own processing and manufacturing operations. However, Northern governments would need to eliminate tariffs on cocoa products and chocolate which currently restrict the import of processed products and inhibit a fairer trading relationship and growers' opportunities for greater returns. Furthermore, with some of the lowest standards in Europe, the UK government could insist on a higher cocoa content in chocolate, thereby benefitting producers and offering consumers a better quality product.

In the long-term, as biotechnological cocoa comes on stream, with the potential to produce 3000 lbs per acre, most cocoa producers will have little chance of maintaining an income from cocoa production. Indeed, if the gene mongers are able to produce their cocoa in the lab, there is no future for any cocoa producer. Growers have no choice but to reduce their dependence on a crop with an increasingly unviable future and to find solutions which are sustainable, rather than struggle to achieve more competitive prices or simply switch to another crop to watch the same pattern happen all over again.

*Long-term Solutions*

Much of the long-term solution to problems examined here rests with regaining a self-sufficiency, rather than producing and exporting to feed a small and privileged market. Farmers now, out of necessity, are resorting to farming crops to feed themselves. Rather than continue to produce crops for export as luxury with little return, farmers could ensure a food security currently lacking. They could reconstruct a viable future utilising their land and skills, rather than hanker after the elusive draw of 'development'. Marketing locally produced food would encourage self-sufficiency and could lead to increased local trading rather than the incessant push towards a global market place.

As the power behind the whole process of chocolate consumption, the chocolate industry is in a position to implement profound changes in the cocoa chain. Indeed, manufacturers have stated that "Producing countries are entitled to fair and remunerative prices in order to guarantee the quality of supplies"[7].

As the priority is to offer consumers choice, the industry could work with the fair trade groups to offer consumers a fair trade and organic line of products. That is, to offer a real choice of alternative product, rather than the choice between 1000 brands all produced under similar conditions and all likely to contain pesticide residues. Indeed, with such influence in the growing regions the industry is in a position to encourage widespread organic production of cocoa.

Shaped by the values of patriarchy, the global abuse of the earth is paralleled by our private abuse of our food and our bodies. Our relationship to food has become distorted in a culture which disempowers women, through awarding value to a prescribed outer appearance. Whilst considered an indulgence, chocolate has become a symbol of the constraint placed upon women to look good and therefore to control their intake of food. To consume with consciousness is to know when we want to eat chocolate (rather than wanting something else, or consuming it with guilt) and is to effect both a personal and political empowerment as we reconsider the relationship we have with our bodies and our food.

**Chocolate Unwrapped** The Politics of Pleasure

Today, presented in a package designed to attract custom on impulse, our relationship with chocolate as consumers has rendered it divorced from any context or understanding beyond the contemporary marketing myth. Purchased and manufactured in an increasingly sophisticated environment, we know relatively little about the circumstances of the origins of our food. Under such circumstances, it is easy to take for granted the endless availability of chocolate, its media-driven mythology and its unassuming price.

The source of the profound inequities and imbalance within our global culture is deep and all pervasive, yet a synthesis of new perspectives offers hope. Environmental perspectives play a crucial role in understanding and reconsidering our relationship with the earth, and new trade and development views challenge the inequity of North South relations.

At the same time feminism has a vital place in challenging the contemporary structures of power. Ecofeminists, in considering the root cause of present problems to stem from a dominant dualistic worldview which is imbalanced and creates inequity, are creating a new paradigm which seeks to challenge the split between men and women, culture and earth, North and South by revaluing that which has been devalued - including women and the earth - and honouring the whole.

To give greater consideration to the process which brings food to our bodies, rather than simply consume the end product, is to eat with consciousness. Such a holistic view is crucial to rekindling a sustainable, healthy and sacred relationship with the earth.

# References

## Introduction
1 Why Women? Gender Issues and Eating Disorders, ed. Bridget Dolan and Inez Gitzinger, European Council on Eating Disorders 1991.

## Chapter 1
1. Middle Classic Meso-America AD 400-700, E. Pasatory; US 1978 p 138.
2. Esotericism in the Popol Vuh; R. Girard; Theosophical University Press, California 1979 p 132.
3. The Ancient Maya, Morley; Stanford University Press California 1956 pp 186 & 221.
4. Ancient Mexico, Peterson; Allen & Unwin London 1959 p 166-180.
5. The Conquest of New Spain (trans.), Bernard Diaz; Penguin 1989 p 226.
6. The Story of Chocolate Information Sheet; Nestlé Co. Ltd.
7. The Story of Cocoa and Chocolate; Cadbury Ltd 1987.
8. History, Rowntree Mackintosh; York 1990.
9. Ibid Cadbury Ltd 1987.
10. Why Hershey is smacking its lips; Business Week Oct 30 1989 p 62.
11. Chocolate Market Review, Cadbury Ltd; Birmingham UK 1991 p 9.
12. Ibid Cadbury Ltd 1991 p 9.
13. The Woman's Encyclopedia of Myths and Secrets, Barbara Walker; Harper Collins San Francisco 1983.
14. Ibid Cadbury Ltd 1991
15. The Cocoa Slaves of Brazil; The Independent Magazine 9 September 1989 p 22.

*Additional Bibliography*
Myths of Pre-Colombian America, Donald A Mackenzie; Gresham London 1945
The Gods of Mexico, L. Spence; T. Fischer Unwin London 1923
Ancient Mexico, Sahagun; Fisk University Press New York 1932.
The Rise and Fall of Maya Civilisation, J.E.S. Thompson; University of

Oklahoma Press USA 1954.

The Maya, Coe; Thames and Hudson 1987.

The Sweet Taste of Success; The Illustrated London News 273 April 1985

# Chapter 2

1. For an example related to Easter see The Times, March 16-22 1985, Company, February 1991.

2. You and Yours, Radio 4, 26 Sept 1991.

3. The Politics of Meat, Carol J Adams; Polity Press 1990.

4. A Market Sector Overview - Confectionery, Keynote Report 1991.

5. The Conquest of New Spain, Bernard Diaz; Penguin May 1991

6. The Complete Herbal New Ed., Nicholas Culpepper; Thomas Kelly & Co.1863.

7. Naughty but Nice: Food Pornography, in Female Desire Rosalind Coward; Paladin 1984

8. CTN Magazine 15/2/91.

9. Independent Television Commission, 70 Brompton Rd.London SW3.

10. Mythologies, Roland Barthes; Paladin 1957.

11. Eating Virtue, The Sociology of Food and Eating; Paul Atkinson; ed. Anne Murcott Gower 1983.

12. For example, see Fat is a Feminist Issue, Susie Orbach; Hamlyn 1979 and Womansize - The Tyranny of Slenderness, Kim Chernin; Women's Press 1983.

13. Statement in speech by Lord Cole, Chairman of Unilever at Unilever AGM 28.4.65.

14. Marketing, 7 March 1991.

15. Chocolate Market Review of 1991, Cadbury Limited.

16. Cocoa to 1993 — A Commodity in Crisis, Economic Intelligence Unit 1987 p 104.

17. Trends in Pharmacological Science Vol 10, October 1989 p 390.

18. The Complete Guide to Advertising, Torin Douglas; MacMillan 1984 p 33

19. Advertising, Rowntree-Mackintosh 11.9.88.

20. Source; MEAL.Statistics Research Organisation.

21. Marketing, 7 March 1991 p 27.
22. The Taste of Chocolate, New Home Economics, Cadbury Ltd.

# Chapter 3
1. See the Observer of 15.11.92 and She Magazine November 1992 as examples from one month's media attention on chocolate.
2. For example, Mary-Jane Rust of the Women's Therapy Centre, London
3. Trends in Pharmacological Science Vol 10 October 1989  p 390.
4. Co-founder of the Women's Therapy Centre and author of Fat is a Feminist Issue 1 & 2; Hamlyn Paperbacks UK 1978 & 1984.
5. The Beauty Myth, Naomi Wolf; Vintage UK 1990.
6. 33,000 Women Tell How They Really Feel About Their Bodies, Glamour, USA, February 1984 (cited in ibid Wolf 1990).
7. Eating Your Heart Out - The Emotional Meaning of Eating Disorders, Julia Buckroyd; Optima UK 1989 p 5.
8. The Golden Cage- The Enigma of Anorexia Nervosa, Hilde Bruch; Open Books 1987.
9. Ibid Buckroyd 1989 p 10.
10. Ibid Wolf 1990 p 183.
11. Why Women? Gender Issues and Eating Disorders, Bridget Dolan and Inez Glitzinger; European Council on Eating Disorders 1991.
12. Ibid Wolf 1990 p 183.
13. Guardian 12.14.91
14. Why Women? Gender Issues and Eating Disorders, Bridget Dolan and Inez Glitzinger; European Council on Eating Disorders 1991.
15. A Womans Place? The Portrayal of Women in Advertisements, Sue Phipps; The Advertising Association 1991 p 9.
16. Ibid Wolf 1990 p 184.

*Additional Bibliography*
Womansize—The Tyranny Of Slenderness, Kim Chernin; The Women's Press UK 1983.

# Chapter 4

1. Cadbury Information Sheet; reprinted from Cadbury's Food Thoughts, the publication prepared for Home Economics teachers by Cadbury's Ltd.

2. Chocolate, Cocoa and Confectionery: Science and Technology, Bernard W Minife, Van Nostrand Reinhold, 1989.

3. Chocolate and Cocoa Manufacture, Dr E H Meursing, Food Technology International 1987.

4. UK Food Labelling Regulations SI 1984/1305; EEC Directive 73/241; British Food Regulations part VIII(b) Confectionery, Sugar and Chocolate 1982

5. ibid Chocolate, Cocoa and Confectionery: Science and Technology, Bernard W Minife 1989.

6. ibid Chocolate, Cocoa and Confectionery: Science and Technology, Bernard W Minife 1989.

7. Butterworth's Food Law, 2nd Supplement Jan 1982; UK Cocoa and Chocolate Regulations SI 1976/541; EEC Directive 73/241.

8. The Politics of Food, Geoffrey Cannon; Century Hutchinson, 1987.

9. E is for Additives, Maurice Hansen, Thorsons 1984.

10. Additives and Children's Diets, London Food Commission 1990.

11. Additive News, Hyperactive Children's Support Group 1992.

12. Food Additives — A Technology Out of Control?, E Millstone; New Scientist 18/10/84

13. A Consumer's Dictionary of Food Additives, R Winter; Crown Publishers New York 1988

14. Danger, Additives at Work, Dr M Miller; London Food Commission 1985.

15. Food Fit for the World, Tim Lang; SAFE Alliance, March 1992 p20.

16. ibid The Politics of Food, Geoffrey Cannon.

17. Healthy Eating — Fact and Fiction, A Bradley et al; Which Books 1989.

18. A handbook of dental health for health visitors, Health Education Authority 1990.

19. A handbook of dental health for health visitors, Health Education Authority 1990.

20. A handbook of dental health for health visitors, Health Education Authority 1990.

21. A handbook of dental health for health visitors, Health Education Authority 1990.

The Scientific Basis of Dental Health Education — A Policy Document, Health Education Authority 1989.

Sugars in the Diet — A Briefing Paper, Health Education Authority 1990

Dietary Sugars and Human Disease, COMA 1989.

22. A handbook of dental health for health visitors, Health Education Authority 1990.

23. ibid The Politics of Food, Geoffrey Cannon &

Healthy Eating — Fact and Fiction, Bradley et al 1989.

24. Food and Health: The Experts Agree, G. Cannon, Consumers Association Ltd, UK 1992.

25. Dietary Reference Values for Food Energy and Nutrients for the UK, COMA, HMSO 1991.

26. Sweetness and Blight BBC Public Eye 22/3/91.

27. The Food Magazine, Oct/Dec 1990.

28. The Guardian Weekend 3.10.92.

29. ibid Healthy Eating — Fact and Fiction, Bradley et al.

30. Britains Deadly Diet, New Scientist 11.5.91.

31. Enjoy Healthy Eating, Health Education Authority 1991;

On the State of Public Ill-Health: Premature Mortality in the UK and Europe, Professor John Catford; British Medical Journal Dec 1984.

32. COMA 1991.

33. Cannon 1992.

34. Letter from Health Education Authority, Nutrition Officer to Women's Environmental Network 30th April 1992

35. ACARD, The Food Industry and Technology, Cabinet Office, Advisory Council for Applied Research and Development, HMSO UK 1982.


*Additional Bibliography*

Confectionery in Perspective, Cocoa, Chocolate and Confectionery Alliance.

Additives and Children's diets, Playgroups Guidance Note; Food Commission.

Food Additives: A Shoppers Guide, Tim Lang and Erik Millstone; Channel 4 TV 1992.

Food Values: Health and Diet, A Sheiham, M Marmot, N Ruck; in British Social Attitudes - 1987 Report ed R Jowell; Gower Publishing Co, Aldershot 1987.

Food and Health:Now and the Future, ed R Cottrell; Parthenon Publishing 1987.

Social Trends, Central Statistical Office 1992.

Family Expenditure Survey, Central Statistical Office 1991.

Look Again at the Label — Chemical Additives in Food, Soil Association, 1984.

# Chapter 5

1. Mail on Sunday; 21 January 1990.

2. The Food Magazine, Oct/Dec 1989 p 19.

3. Residues found in Cadbury's Bournville Plain, Mars' Galaxy, Nestle's Yorkie, and Suchard's Milka Praline Crisp

4. ibid The Food Magazine; Oct/Dec 1989 p 19

5. Evaluated by statisticians, the diet is divided into 20 groups of food and representative quantities of each of the 115 comprising items are calculated for the test. Tests were carried out on seven groups of food in 1966, 1970 and 1974, rearranged into nine groups for testing in 1975 and 1979, and then revised into 20 groups for tests in 1981, 1984, and 1989 which will be carried out every five years in future: Food Surveillance Paper 9, MAFF; HMSO 1982 p6-9.

6. It examines between 40-70 out of the 400 approved pesticides in the UK: Poisoned Harvest: A Consumers Guide To Use And Abuse, Christopher Robbins; Victor Gollancz 1991 p 132; Food Surveillance Paper 23, MAFF; HMSO UK 1988 p30-35.

7. Ibid Poisoned Harvest: A Consumers Guide To Use And Abuse, Christopher Robbins 1991 p 126.

8. Food Surveillance Paper 9, MAFF; HMSO UK, 1982, p 7

9. Letter to WEN from MAFF Food Safety Directorate 6 1 92, citing tests on

cocoa and cocoa butter for ethylene oxide by the Working Party on Pesticide Residues in 1980.

10. AGCHEM, British Agrochemicals Association, UK; Jan/March 1991 p1.

11. ibid AGCHEM 1991.

12. P is for Pesticides, Tim Lang, Charlie Clutterbuck; Ebury Press London 1991 p 42.

13. MAFF Research Consultative Document Pesticides Sub Group 1988.

14. The Pesticides (Maximum Residue Levels in Food) Regulations 1988/1378.

15. PAN Europe Newsletter Vol 6 no 19 1991.

16. The Future of Australian Food Standards, A preliminary analysis of current and proposed standards for pesticide residues in food, Australian Consumers' Association; Australia June 1991.

17. Food Fit for the World - A Discussion Paper, Tim Lang SAFE Alliance; March 1992.

18. Information available from London Food Commission, address 5-11 Worship Street London EC2.

19. ibid P is for Pesticides, Tim Lang, Charlie Clutterbuck; 1991.

20 . Letter to Dr A Hay, Dept.Chemical Pathology, Leeds University from BCCCA 18/4/89.

21. ibid Letter to Dr A Hay, from BCCCA 18/4/89.

22. Letter to WEN from BCCCA 19/8/91.

23. ibid Letter to Dr.A Hay from BCCCA 18/4/89.

24. ibid Letter to Dr.A Hay from BCCCA 18/4/89.

25. Letter to WEN from BCCCA 19/8/91.

26. The Pesticide Handbook, Peter Hurst, Alastair Hay, Nigel Dudley; Journeyman 1991.

27. Letter to Food Commission from Cadbury 17/5/89.

28. ibid Poisoned Harvest: A Consumers Guide To Use And Abuse, Christopher Robbins; Victor Gollancz 1991.

29. Letter to WEN from BCCCA 19/8/91.

30. Based on assumptions of an adult weighing 70 kg eating 50 g (the size of a small block of chocolate) each day. The average residue in chocolate (at 25ppb level) would be around .0003mg - less than 1% of the acceptable daily

intake of 0.008 mg/kg bodyweight /day.

31. Letter to Food Commission from Cadbury 17/5/89.

32. ibid Poisoned Harvest: A Consumers Guide To Use And Abuse, Christopher Robbins; 1991 p 119.

33. ibid P is for Pesticides, Tim Lang Charlie Cliutterbuck; 1991 p 80.

34. The Effects of Pesticides on Human Health, Vol 1 Report and Proceedings of the Agricultural Committee. Second Special Report. session 1986-7. House of Commons HMSO 1987.cited in ibid Poisoned Harvest: A Consumers Guide To Use And Abuse, Christopher Robbins; 1991 p78.

35. ibid P is for Pesticides, Tim Lang Charlie Cliutterbuck; 1991 p79

36. PAN Dirty Dozen Fact Sheets; USA 1991.

37. Pesticide Health and Safety Policy in the UK — A Flawed and Limited Approach? A. Watterson; Journal of Public Health Policy, Winter 1990, p492.

38. ibid P is for Pesticides, Tim Lang Charlie Cliutterbuck; 1991.

39. Carcinogenic - causing cancer, mutagenic - causing genetic damage which is transmitted through the generations,
teratogenic - affecting the foetus.

40. Science, Ames et al; 17 April 1987.

41. Science, S. Epstein; 20 May 1988.

42. The Israeli Breast Cancer Anomaly, JB Westin and E Richter: Ann. NYAS 609, 1990 pp 269-79, cited in Profiting from Cancer—Vested Interests and the Cancer Epidemic, S. Epstein; The Ecologist Vol 22 No 5 Sept/Oct 1992.

43. Regulation of chemical carcinogens, US Regulatory Council; Washington DC US GPO 1979 cited in ibid Poisoned Harvest: A Consumers Guide To Use And Abuse, Christopher Robbins; 1991 p 77.

44. For Our Kids Sake, : How to Protect Your Child Against Pesticides in Food, Mothers And Others For Pesticide Limits; Natural Resources Defense Council US 1989.

45. Profiting from Cancer—Vested Interests and the Cancer Epidemic, S. Epstein; The Ecologist Vol 22 No 5 Sept/Oct 1992.

46. Intolerable Risk: Pesticides in our Children's Food, Natural Resources Defense Council, US 1989.

47.ibid Poisoned Harvest: A Consumers Guide To Use And Abuse,

Christopher Robbins; 1991 p 124.

48. Food Surveillance Paper 23, MAFF; HMSO UK 1989 p 60.

49. ibid Food Surveillance Paper 23, MAFF; HMSO UK 1989 p6

50. Food Surveillance Paper 16, MAFF; HMSO UK 1986 p 9.and Review of the Insecticide Lindane for Submission to the World Bank Pesticide Advisory Panel, Dr Paul Johnson; Greenpeace International 1989.

51. Pesticide Outlook, August 1990 pp 10-15.

52. Review of the Insecticide Lindane for Submission to the World Bank Pesticide Advisory Panel, Dr Paul Johnson; Greenpeace International 1989.

53. ibid For Our Kids Sake, Natural Resources Defense Council; 1989 p 73.

54. EPA Pesticide Residue Surveillance results in 1988.

55. The Manufacturing Confectioner, US September 1991 pp 97-104.


*Additional Bibliography*

Pesticides and Your Food: How to Reduce The Risks To Your Health, Andrew Watterson; Green Print 1991.

British Medical Association Pesticide Report; BMA, 1990.

The Residue Report: Action Plan for Safer Food, Stephanie Lashford; Thorsons 1988.

The Soil Association Handbook, Nigel Dudley; Optima 1991.

Pesticide Users' Health and Safety Handbook, Andrew Watterson; Gower Technical 1988

# Chapter 6

1. Cocoa 4th Ed. GAR Wood, RA Lass; Longman Scientific 1985.

**WEST AFRICA**

1. Cacao in West Africa, L. A. Are, D. R. G. Gwynne-Jones; Oxford University Press 1974.

2. Ibid L. A. Are, D. R. G. Gwynne-Jones 1974.

3. Quarterly Bulletin of Cocoa Statistics, Vol XVII No 4, ICCO; London 1991.

4. A History of West Africa, J. D. Fage; Cambridge University Press 1969 p 192-5.

5. The Emergence of Capitalist relations in South Asante Cocoa Farming c

# References

1916-33, P. Austin; Journal of African History 28 1987 p 259-79.

6. Quarterly Bulletin of Cocoa Statistics, Vol XVII No 4 1991; ICCO London.

7. Role of Women in Cocoa Production, M. Breedvelt, J. Sol; InZet 1992.

8. Ibid M. Breedvelt, J Sol 1992.

9. Cocoa and Chaos in Ghana, G Mikell; Paragon House New York 1989.

10. Ibid G. Mikell 1989.

11. International Federation of Plantation Agricultural and Allied Workers News 7-8.89.

12. The IMF and Ghana: The Confidential Report, Eboe Hutchful; Zed 1987.

13. W. Keeling, Financial Times 12.6.91.

14. W. Keeling, Financial Times 6.4.89.

15. The World Bank, the International Bank for Reconstruction and Development, was established in 1944 to expand the global economy. It makes long-term loans to Third World governments, to implement projects aimed at promoting Western style economic development. Many loans for large projects like mines, hydroelectric dams, bridges and roads would then facilitate private investment. The environmental effects of many of these massive projects have caused great alarm. Critical investigation has further shown that World Bank projects rarely reduce poverty.

The IMF was created at the same time as the World Bank, to stabilise exchange rates between currencies and regulate the world monetary system. It gives short-term loans designed to solve balance of payment problems and demands severe austerity policies in return. It has also been criticised on environmental and poverty grounds. In response to the 1982 international banking crisis when Mexico threatened to default on debt repayment, the IMF offered to reschedule many debts, but, in return, made stringent demands for drastic restructuring of the economies of the debtor countries. In 1990 world debt is nearly double the 1982 figure of US$802 billion.

Both institutions are controlled by votes weighted according to contributions. The US has around 20% of the vote in each case and the main industrial countries generally have control of decision making. See: Pinstripes and Poverty: Inside the World Bank New Internationalist December 1990; Third World First factsheet 2 Aid; Aid: Rhetoric and Reality, Teresa Hayter and

Catherine Watson; Pluto Press 1985.

16. Rising Star of Africa, V Brittain; Guardian 17.12.88.

17. Cocoa Addicts, J Tanner; New Internationalist February 1990.

18. International Conference on Pesticides and Cocoa Production; TIE, Amsterdam 1988.

19. Woodsworth, Financial Times 22.6.88.

20. Ibid International Conference on Pesticides and Cocoa Production 1988.

21. Ibid Woodsworth 22.6.88.

22. Women and the World Economic Crisis, J. Vickers; Zed Books London 1991 Ch. 9.

23. Ibid V. Brittain 17.12.88.

24. Ghana profile, New Internationalist June 1987 p 32.

25. Quarterly Bulletin of Cocoa Statistics, Vol XVII No 4 1991; ICCO London.

26. The Trade Trap: Poverty and The Global Commodity Markets, Belinda Coote; Oxfam 1992.

27. Third World Debt, A Christian Aid briefing paper on commercial bank tax relief and the Trinidad terms, Christian Aid 1990.

28. Economic Policy Institute of Washington Report, cited in Third World Economics 16-30 Sept 1991 p 11.

29. New Internationalist, December 1990.

30. Food First, Frances Moor Lappe and Joseph Collins Souvenir Press 1980.

31. New Internationalist, December 1990.

32. A Legacy for My Children, A. Yeboah-Afari; New Internationalist November 1991.


*Additional Bibliography*

Plunder In Ghana's Rainforest for Illegal Profit, Friends Of The Earth UK 1992.

Cocoa (4th Edn), G. A. R. Wood, R. A. Lass,; Longman Scientific UK 1985.

Journal of African History 29, D. Meredith 1988.

Cocoa Conflicts, Food Matters Worldwide No 6 May 1990.

W Keeling, Financial Times 24.8.90.

V Brittain, Guardian 15.6.84.

# References

Public Policies and the Misuse of Forest Resources, R. Repetto & M. Gillis, World Resources Institute US 1988.
The Global Chocolate Factory, TIE Amsterdam 1990.

BRAZIL

1. Middle America - Its land and Peoples, R West; Prentice Hall USA 1976.
2. Cocoa in Brazil, Cocoa Growers Bulletin No 23, R. A. Lass W. M. Aitken; Cadbury September 1975.
3. Ibid Food Matters Worldwide No 6 May 1990.
4. Cocoa and Coffee International Issue 1 1992.
5. Brazil - Farming Out Of Debt, Food Matters Worldwide October 1989.
6. Ibid Food Matters Worldwide October 1989.
7. Ibid TIE 1990.
8. Ibid TIE 1987 p 3.
9. The Cocoa Slaves of Brazil, The Independent Magazine 9.9.89.
10. Ibid Food Matters Worldwide October 1989.
11. Financial Times 21.11.90.
12. The Global Chocolate Factory, Transnational Information Exchange Amsterdam 1990 p 9.
13. Report of International Cocoa Workers Meeting, Transnational Information Exchange Amsterdam 1987.
14. The Cocoa Slaves of Brazil, The Independent Magazine 9.9.89.
15. Financial Times 18.6.91.
16. Cocoa Conflicts, Food Matters Worldwide No 6 May 1990.
17. Ibid TIE 1987.
18. The Resistance of the Cocoa Workers, CEAS Rural Team, CEPLAC Brazil 1985.
19. Interview with Carlinhos, Trade Union President of Garotto chocolate factory in Espirito Santo State 15.2.92.
20. Ibid Carlinhos interview and Programme of Activities Related to the Question of Rural Worker Women - 1992, CONTAG Brazil 1992.
21. Spare Rib March 1990.
22. Medio Ambiente y Poblacion; una vision critica, Thais Corral; Brazil 1992.

23. Ibid Carlinhos interview.
24. Vanette Almeida, rural workers leader from North East Brazil speaking at The Brazil Network National launch of the Chico Mendez Solidarity Fund, London 15.2.92.
25. Ibid TIE 1990.
26. Celso, Trade Union President of Chadler Cocoa plant in Salvador, Bahia, speaking at The Brazil Network National launch of the Chico Mendez Solidarity Fund, London 15.2.92.
27. Financial Times 18.6.91.

*Additional Bibliography*
The Spanish Seaborn Empire, J. H. Parry; 1966.
The Ecologist Vol 17 4/5 1987 p 157.
Plantations and Planes, Sue Branford; New Internationalist February 1990.
Bahia Cocoa Conference, The Manufacturing Confectioner; April 1987.
Brazil, Amnesty International Briefing, 1988.
The Land Problem In Brazil, Francis McDonagh; Catholic Institute of International Relations 1992.


MALAYSIA
1. Women in the Plantation Sector, SIMBA Newsletter September 1991.
2. Suara No. 6, Sahabat Alam Malaysia 1987.
3. Tamils currently account for 64% of the current workforce: author's communication with Mr Varatharajoo of Sahabat Alam Malaysia Kuala Lumpur.
4. Ibid Sahabat Alam Malaysia 1987.
5. The Women's Burden, Far Eastern Economic Review 7 June 1990 p 18.
6. Human Resources Ministry 1989. cited in New Sunday Times, Malaysia 6.5.90.
7. New Sunday Times, Malaysia 6.5.90.
8. Ibid SIMBA Newsletter September 1991.
9. Ibid Sahabat Alam Malaysia 1987.
10. Ibid Far Eastern Economic Review 7 June 1990.
11. Utusan Konsumer, Consumers' Association Malaysia February 1990.
12. Links 29/30, Third World First 1987.

13. Utusan Konsumer, Consumers' Association Malaysia May 1990.

14. Sixth Malaysia Plan 1991-1995, Government of Malaysia.

15. New Straits Times, Malaysia 11.1.89.

16. Public Policies and the Misuse of Forest Resources, Repetto & Gillis; World Resources Institute USA 1988 p 155.

17. Malaysian Cocoa Outlook, Federal Agricultural Marketing Authority Malaysia May 1990.

18. Ibid Repetto & Gillis. add figures removed from original text.

19. Daily Star Malaysia 4.6.91.

20. Ibid Sixth Malaysia Plan pp 92 and 107.

21      Ibid Sixth Malaysia Plan.

22. The Global Chocolate Factory, Transnational Information Exchange Amsterdam 1990.

23. Sime Darby's agricultural division made M$435.7 million (£80 million) in 1990: Sime Derby Annual Report 1990.

24. A World Bank loan of US$71.5 million in 1989 is resettling 9,000 families on 61,000 hectares in Sabah to plant tree crops: World Bank News April 27 1989.

25. Ibid Sixth Malaysia Plan .

26. Forest Destruction in South East Asia, Phil Hurst; Ecologist vol 17 4/5 1987 p 170.

27. Women Farmers and Rural Change in Asia, Noeleen Heyzer; Asia and Pacific Development Centre Kuala Lumpur Malaysia 1987 pp 163-219.

28. Business Times, Malaysia 7.3.1990.

29. New Straits Times, Malaysia 23.4.1990.


INDONESIA

1. Financial Times, 18.3.88.

2. Environesia, WALHI Indonesia December 1989.

3. Asian-Pacific Environment Vol 5 no 4, APPEN Malaysia February 1989 p 11.

4. Down To Earth vol 1  Feb 1989.

5. Down to Earth vol 4, August 1989 p 10.

6. Jakarta Post, Indonesia 13.1.92.

7. Down to Earth no 5, October 1989 p 9.

8. Down to Earth No 11, November 1990.

9. Whose Hand on the Chainsaw?, UK Government Policy and the Tropical Rainforests, Friends of the Earth, October 1992.

10. Setiakawan No4-5, WALHI, Indonesia January-June 1990 p 22.

11. The Ecologist Vol 16 No 2/3 1986.

12. Siberut Island, Indonesia, SOS Siberut 1992.

13. Down to Earth No 2, April 1989.

14. Public Policies and the Misuse of Forest Resources, Repetto and Gillis; World Resources Institute USA 1988 p 45.

15. The Environmental Impact of Transmigration, Charles Secrett; ibid The Ecologist p 80.

16. ibid Public Policies and the Misuse of Forest Resources, Repetto and Gillis; World Resources Institute USA 1988 p45.

# Chapter 7

1. Acute Pesticide Poisoning - A Major Problem, J Jeyaratnam; World Health Statistics Quarterly vol 43 1990 pp 139-144.

2. Dirty Dozen Fact Sheet, Pesticide Action Network 1985.

3. Public Health Impact of Pesticides Used In Agriculture, WHO/UNEP, Geneva, in preparation cited in Acute Pesticide Poisoning: A Major Global Health Problem, J Jeyaratnam; World Health Statistics Quarterly 43(3) 1990 p 139-144.

4. Victims Without Voice, Vasanthi Arumugam; Tenaganita & Pesticide Action Network Asia & Pacific, Malaysia 1992.

5. The Independent 18.3.91.

6. International Agricultural Development; January/February 1990 p 5.

7. The Pesticide Hazard, B Dinham Zed 1993 p 82.

8. Cocoa 4th ed, GAR Wood RA Lass; Longman Scientific & Technical p 96 and Manufacturing Confectioner Sept 1991 p 102.

9. The Pesticide Hazard, B Dinham; Zed 1993 p 173.

10. The Malaysian Experience, Chee Yoke Ling; Women Environment

Development Seminar Report, Women's Environmental Network March 1989 p 23.

11. ibid Victims Without Voice, Vasanthi Arumugam; Tenaganita & Pesticide Action Network Asia & Pacific, Malaysia 1992.

12. Ibid Vasanthi Arumugam 1992.

13. New Straits Times, Malaysia 4.6.90.

14. New Straits Times, Malaysia 14.8.91

15. Ibid Vasanthi Arumugam 1992.

16. Paraquat and Occupational Hazards, Barbara Dinham; Pesticide News No 16, Pesticide Trust June 1992.

17. Dirty Dozen Campaigner, Pesticide Action Network USA September 1989 p 1.

18. Ibid TIE September 1988 p 13.

19. Import and Export Statistics, Business Monitor 1987.

20. The Cocoa Slaves of Brazil; The Independent Magazine, September 1989.

21. Ibid TIE September 1988.

22. Summary of Report on Pesticides on Cocoa in Ghana, Patrick Aculey; Cocoa Research Institute Ghana.

23. Ibid TIE September 1988 p 8.

24. Ibid Patrick Aculey DATE.

25. Ibid TIE September 1988 p 8.

26. Ibid Pesticide Action Network Dirty Dozen Fact Sheet 1990.

27. Chain of Poison: Lindane Production in Spain, Topsy Jewell; Greenpeace International 1989.

28. Dirty Dozen Campaigner Pesticide Action Network USA May 1989 p 6.

29. Pesticides UK 1990.Keynote Report; Keynote Publications 1990

30. AGROW 1 June 1990.

31. Agrow No 163 10.7.92 pp 19-20.

32. The Control of Pests and Pesticides Broad Sheet, Pesticide Trust.

33. Dirty Dozen Campaigner; Pesticide Action Network USA January 1990.

34. Transnationals Information Exchange (TIE), International Conference on Pesticides and Cocoa Production; Netherlands September 1988.

35. Pesticides will be placed on the PIC register if they meet one of three cri-

teria - if a chemical is banned in 5 or more countries on health or environmental grounds, if a chemical is banned or severely restricted in 1 country on
similar grounds after January 1992, or if it causes health or environmental
problems under conditions of use in developing countries. This list currently
includes pesticides such as paraquat and parathion.
36. The Pesticide Hazard, B Dinham; Zed 1993 p4.

*Additional Bibliography*
Dirty Dozen Fact Sheet Pesticide Action Network USA 1990
Silent Spring, Rachel Carson; Houghton Mifflin USA 1962
This Poisoned Earth: The Truth about Pesticides, Nigel Dudley; Piatkus
Publishers London 1987
P is for Pesticides, Tim Lang and Charlie Clutterbuck; Ebury Press
London 1991
Pesticide Users' Health And Safety Handbook, Andrew Watterson; Gower
Technical Publishers UK 1988
A Growing Problem: Pesticides and the Third World Poor, David Bull; Oxfam
UK 1982
Circle of Poison, David Weir and Mark Shapiro; Institute of Food Policy
USA 1981
The Pesticide Handbook, Peter Hurst, Alistair Hay and Nigel Dudley;
Journeyman 1991.

# Chapter 8

1. Quarterly Bulletin of Cocoa Statistics, XVII No4 ICCO 1991 (1990/91 -
2,507,000 tonnes).
2. Cocoa to 1993: A Commodity in Crisis, Economic Intelligence Unit 1989.
3. ibid ICCO 1991.
4. ibid Economic Intelligence Unit 1989.
5. ibid ICCO 1991 (consumption: 2,079,000 tonnes of cocoa).
6. New Straits Times, Malaysia 17.4.92 (1.5 million tonnes of cocoa).
7. Merchants of Drink - Transnational Control of World Beverages, Frederick

Clairmonte, John Cavanagh; Third World Network, Malaysia 1988 p 59.

8. Business Week 11.12.85 cited in ibid Clairmonte and Cavanagh 1988 p 74.

9. Corporate profile published by E D & F Mann Group.

10. Marketing and Distribution System for Cocoa, UNCTAD, Geneva 1973, cited in ibid Clairmonte and Cavanagh 1988 p 62.

11. Cocoa Conflicts, Food Matters Worldwide No 6 May 1990.

12. The Trade Trap - Poverty and the Global Commodity Markets, Belinda Coote; Oxfam 1992.

13. Financial Times 21.8.89.

14. The Independent 13.10.89.

15. Financial Times 4.1.89.

16. Financial Times 6.9.91.

17. Third World Economics, Third World Network; Malaysia 16-30 September 1991.

18. ibid Economic Intelligence Unit 1989.

19. ibid TIE 1989.

20. ibid TIE 1989.

21. ibid ICCO 1991.

22. ibid Economic Intelligence Unit 1989.

23. Financial Times 6.9.91.

24. The Global Chocolate Factory, TIE Amsterdam 1989.

25. Coffee and Cocoa International, Issue 4 1988.

26. SOMO is an Amsterdam-based organisation which researches transnational companies and has investigated the chocolate companies. See also ibid TIE 1989 p 18.

27. Financial Times Belize Survey 16.10.85.

28. Malaysian Business 16.11.86.

29. Financial Times 7.7.89.

30. Cocoa Growers Bulletin, Cadbury December 1989.

31. Financial Times 24.5.85.

32. Financial Times 30.9.92.

33. Nestlé Annual Report 1989.

34. The Worldwide Cocoa Trade, Nestlé.

35. Philip Morris Annual Report 1990.

36. ibid Economic Intelligence Unit 1989.

37. Life on Mars; Independent on Sunday 26.7.92.

38. Cadbury-Schweppes Annual Report 1990.

39. Financial Times Food Survey 5.3.90.

40. Financial Times 24.6.88.

41. Keynote Report, Confectionery 1991.

42. Financial Times 30.9.92.

43. ibid Economic Intelligence Unit 1989.

44. Manufacturing Confectioner, US January 1992.

45. Rowntree Company Information Sheet.

46. ibid Nestlé Annual Report 1989.

47. ibid Nestlé Annual Report 1989.

48. A Tradition of Excellence, Hershey Foods.

49. The top company, Lotte, made sales worth over US$ one and a half billion in 1990, closely followed by Meiji, Morinaga, Glico and Fujiya Japanscan 1990.

50. Ibid Economic Intelligence Unit 1989.

51. Jacobs Suchard Annual Report 1989: distribution companies in Japan, Hong Kong, South Korea and Singapore and licensees in Thailand, Malaysia, Indonesia and Korea.

52. Manufacturing Confectioner, US November 1991.

53. Manufacturing Confectioner, US January 1991.

# Chapter 9

1. Genetic Engineering and Food, doc.EN\V\119511, The Greens; European Parliament.

2. Theobroma is the genus of the cocoa tree of which there are over 20 species. Theobroma Cacao is the only widely cultivated one.

3. Cracking the Cocoa Bean, Penn State Agriculture; USA Fall 1986.

4. Dr. Paul J. Fritz head of the research programme quoted in Cracking the

Cocoa Bean, Penn State Agriculture Fall 1986.

5. Biotechnology - An Activists Handbook, The Vermont Biotechnology Working Group USA 1991 p 9.

6. Lester Brown of the World Watch Institute in Washington DC quoted in State of the World 1990; Worldwatch Institute USA 1990.

7. The Ecologist Vol 21 No 5 Sept-Oct 1991.

8. Genetic Engineering, The Genetics Forum 1990.

9. 13th report The Release of genetically modified organisms to the Environment, Royal Commission on Environmental Pollution; HMSO July 1989.

10. Biotechnology - Applications to the Cocoa Plant, Fritz, Fanji and Stetler; Cacao Biotechnology USA 1986.

11. Cracking the Cocoa Bean, Penn State Agriculture Fall 1986.

12. Miracle or Menace, Biotechnology and the Third World, Robert Walgate; Panos Institute p 60.

13. The Chocolate Crop, Biotechnology and the Future of World Agriculture , Hobbelink;

14. RAFI Communiqué, Cacao and Biotechnology, Hope Shand; Rural Advancement Fund International USA 1987.

15. ibid RAFI Communiqué, Cacao and Biotechnology.

16. The Manufacturing Confectioner USA May 1991.

17. ibid Biotechnology and the Future of World Agriculture, Hobbelink p 87. & Biotechnology and the current shift in the world's cocoa production; Biotechnology and Development Monitor No.10, March 1992 pp 12-13.

18. ibid RAFI Communiqué, Cacao and Biotechnology.

19. ibid Miracle or Menace, Biotechnology and the Third World.

20. ibid Miracle or Menace, Biotechnology and the Third World.

21. Bioprocessing Technology USA April 1987. Cited in RAFI Communiqué, Cacao and Biotechnology.

22. Biotechnology and the Future of World Agriculture, Hobbelink   p94.

23. ibid RAFI Communiqué, Cacao and Biotechnology.

24. Cell Culture System to Produce Less Costly Vanilla, Bioprocessing Technology, USA January 1991 p 7 cited in RAFI Communique, Update -

Vanilla and Biotechnology Rural Advancement Fund International USA July 1991.

*Additional Bibliography*
Factory Farm, Development Dialogue 1-2,　1988 pp 94-111.
Generation Games - Genetic Engineering and the Future For Our Lives, Pat Spallone; Women's Press 1992.
Hunger Aus Dem Genlabor, Biotechnologie, Dritte Welt und die Rolle der Schweiz, Helen Zweifel; Erklarung von Bern, Switzerland 1989.
Chemists, Geneticists Tinker with Chocolate, Business Times, Malaysia 24.2.89.
Malaysia Cocoa Bean Quality Development, The Manufacturing Confectioner; USA May 1991.

# Chapter 10

1. OS3 News Sheet, OS3, Byfangstrassse 19, 2552 Orpund, Switzerland, June 1991.
2. Cacao - El Ceibo, OS3 Information, Switzerland, January 1990.
3. Statement by Patrick Aculey of the Cocobod, Ghana in letter to WEN 22.5.92.
4. Pesticides News, The Journal of the Pesticides Trust, Thirteenth issue October 1991.
5. Silent Spring, Rachel Carson; Houghton Mifflin, New York 1962.
6. Statement by Sarojini Rengam, Director of Pesticide Action Network Asia and the Pacific, Malaysia. April 1992.
7. Jacobs Suchard Annual Report 1989 p 19.

# Appendix 1

## Table of health and environmental effects of pesticides known to be used on cocoa

### Aldrin*
*Acute effects*
Highly toxic if inhaled, swallowed or absorbed through skin. Nausea, vomiting, hyper-excitability convulsions and/or coma followed by death due to failure of respiratory system [1].
*Chronic effects*
Accumulates in fatty tissue. May cause liver or kidney damage in animals. Probable human carcinogen, possible teratogen [1].
*Environmental effects*
Insecticide. May be highly toxic to fish, freshwater invertebrates and birds. Affects reproduction in wildlife species. Fish and shellfish deaths and population reductions have been observed [1].
As at 1992 aldrin was banned in 39 countries and severely restricted in 14.

### Benomyl
*Acute effects*
Skin rashes and allergen. Slight eye irritant [4].
*Chronic effects*
Possible mutagen, teratogen and carcinogen in animals. Liver changes in animals. Possible embryotoxic in animals [5].
*Environmental effects*
Relatively stable and persistent in the environment. Toxic to a broad spectrum of fungi. Has low mammalian toxicity.

### BHC
*Acute effects*
Eye, skin and throat irritation, headaches, nausea, aplastic anaemia [3].

*Chronic effects*
Some liver changes. May affect eyes, central nervous system, blood and skin. Chronic dermatitis [1]. Suspected carcinogen [5].
*Environmental effects*
Dangerous to bees, harmful to fish and livestock [2].

## Carbaryl
*Acute effects*
Nausea, vomiting, stomach cramps, dimness of vision, difficulty in breathing, skin irritation, weakness, nasal discharge, convulsions [4].
*Chronic effects*
Liver and kidney changes. Weak mutagen. Low mammalian toxicity [4].
*Environmental effects*
Broad spectrum insecticide. Dangerous to honey bees and harmful to fish [2].

## Chlordane
*Acute effects*
Eye and skin irritant, mild dizziness, headaches, weakness, blurred vision, confusion, coughs, vomiting, diarrohea and convulsions[4].
*Chronic effects*
Blood disorders, serious liver and kidney damage in animals. Animal carcinogen[4]. Probable human carcinogen, mutagen, teratogen [1].
*Environmental effects*
Is a contact and stomach poison. Toxic to a wide range of insects. Persistent and bio-accumulative. May produce secondary chronic effects in exposed organisms. Highly toxic to aquatic organisms and birds. Its half-life in soil is four years; soil residues have been detected 14 years after application[1].
As at 1992 chlordane was banned in 30 countries and severely restricted in 12.

## Copper Fungicides
*Acute effects*
Stomach pains, nausea and diarrohea, cough, shortness of breath, weak-

ness, weight loss, lung, liver and kidney disorders. Anaemia, damages immune system. Death[3].

*Chronic effects*

Possible carcinogen. Haemolytic anaemia, dermatitis and skin burns. Eye ulcers[3].

*Environmental effects*

Copper sulphate mixtures are dangerous to bees and harmful to fish and livestock and animals[4].

## Cypermethrin

*Acute Effects*

Skin and eye irritant[2].

*Chronic Effects*

Possible immune suppressant. Possible neurotoxic effects in animals. Possible animal carcinogen[4].

*Environmental effects*

Dangerous to bees. Extremely dangerous to fish[4].

## Dalapon

*Acute effects*

Skin and eye irritation[4].

*Chronic effects*

Possible affects on kidneys[4].

*Environmental effects*

No data.

## Dicrotophos

*Acute effects*

Skin and eye irritant[4].

*Chronic effects*

Possible mutagen. Respiratory paralysis. Possible animal teratogen[4].

*Environmental effects*

Highly toxic. Very toxic especially to honey bees[4].

## Dieldrin*

*Acute effects*

Headache, dizziness, nausea, vomiting, sweating, limb-jerking, convulsions, coma, death[4].

*Chronic effects*

Probable human carcinogen. Animal teratogen. Probable embryotoxic in animals. May reduce male and female fertility[1].

*Environmental effects*

Extremely persistent bio-acumulative insecticide. Eliminated slowly. Effects reproduction in wildlife species. Fish and shellfish deaths and population reductions have been observed. Has been found in human tissue and in mothers' milk[4].

As at 1992 dieldrin was banned in 42 countries and severely restricted in 16.

## Endosulfan

*Acute effects*

Skin rashes, central nervous system stimulant, convulsions, vomiting, weakness, confusion, anorexia, hyperactivity, irritability, dizziness, headaches[4].

*Chronic effects*

Possible human carcinogen and mutagen. Positive human teratogen. Liver and kidney changes in animals. Possible kidney and blood changes[4].

*Environmental effects*

Highly toxic to fish, harmful to bees, dangerous to livestock. Moderately persistent[2].

## Endrin

*Acute effects*

Convulsions, stupor, headache, dizziness, nausea, abdominal discomfort, rapid high fever, lethargy, tremors[4]. Death[1].

*Chronic effects*

Liver, kidney, heart, lung and spleen damage in animals and changes in blood and effects on central nervous system. Possible animal carcinogen. Positive mutagen. Suspect teratogen and embryotoxic in animals and humans[1].

*Environmental effects*

Extremely persistent bioacumulative insecticide. Effects reproduction in wildlife species. Fish and shellfish deaths and population reductions have been observed. High mammalian toxicity[1].

As at 1992 endrin was banned in 39 countries and severely restricted in 8.

## Fenitrothion

*Acute effects*

In animals causes tremor, convulsions, muscular twitching, respiratory paralysis, change in conditioned reflexes[4].

*Chronic effects*

No data on chronic effects[4].

*Environmental effects*

General purpose agricultural insecticide. Moderately toxic. Dangerous to bees. Harmful to fish, livestock, game, animals and wild birds[4].

## Heptachlor

*Acute effects*

Affects central nervous system, causes hyperexcitability, nausea, vomiting, convulsions, depression and death[1].

*Chronic effects*

Possible human carcinogen, teratogen. Affects reproductive system. Effects on blood[1].

*Environmental effects*

Bio-accumulative. Potentially very toxic to fish, freshwater invertebrates and birds. Heptachlor residues have been found in milk[1].

As at 1992 heptachlor was banned in 33 countries and severely restricted in 8.

## Lindane

*Acute effects*

Vomiting and diarrohea followed by convulsions. Causes headaches, nausea, dizziness and tremors, muscular weakness, irritation of eyes, nose and throat. Affects central nervous system, causes hyper-excitability[1,4].

*Chronic effects*
Probable human carcinogen[1]. Positive mutagen. Possible animal teratogen. Affects reproductive system. Animal embryotoxic. In animals causes anaemia, immunity disturbance, changes in liver, kidneys and nasal mucous membranes. Affects central nervous system in animals and humans. Changes in oral cavity and jaw found in animals and humans[4].

*Environmental effects*
Lindane residues have been found worldwide as transfer by evaporation is the most common means of environmental contamination. Lindane and its products have the potential to contaminate surface and groundwater. Slightly to moderately toxic to birds, highly toxic to some aquatic organisms and highly toxic to honey bees and certain beneficial insects. Has been found to bioaccumulate in human fatty tissues and to magnify through the food chain[1].

As at 1992 lindane was banned in 15 countries and severely restricted in 10.

## Malathion

*Acute effects*
Affects cholinesterase. Causes weakness, headaches, nausea, blurred vision, staggering walk, slurred speech, vomiting, diarrohea and uncontrolled urination, shaking muscles, difficulty breathing. Death[4].

*Chronic effects*
Positive animal carcinogen and mutagen. Tests on animals show inhibitor effects on reproduction, food intake and weight. Possible animal teratogen[4].

*Environmental effects*
Highly toxic to honey bees and beneficial insects on contact and harmful to fish but low mammalian toxicity[4].

## Mancozeb

*Acute effects*
Skin and eye irritant. Affects respiratory system[4].

*Chronic effects*
Probable human and animal carcinogen[2]. Possible animal teratogen[4].

*Environmental effects*
Harmful to fish[4].

## Maneb
*Acute effects*
Skin, eye and respiratory tract irritant. Allergic dermatitis. May affect liver[4].
*Chronic effects*
In animals affects thyroid, liver and other organs. Animal carcinogen in lungs.
Effects reproductive system. Probable human carcinogen[2]. possible animal
teratogen[4].
*Environmental effects*
Harmful to poultry and game, toxic to fish[4].

## Methyl bromide
*Acute effects*
Skin and eye irritant. Headaches, nausea, weakness, blurred vision, insom-
nia, convulsion. Central nervous System depressant. Death. If death does
not occur person may remain severely disabled[4].
*Chronic effects*
No data.
*Environmental effects*
Mutagenic. Major depleter of ozone layer. Dangerous to wild birds, animals,
bees and fish[2].

## Parathion
*Acute effects*
Affects blood, liver and kidney function. Causes small pupils, nasal dis-
charges, muscle contractions, headaches, weakness, laryngeal spasms,
anorexia, cramps, diarrohea, convulsions and paralysis. Death[4].
*Chronic effects*
Possible animal carcinogen. Probable animal mutagen. Animal teratogen and
embryotoxic. Growth retardation and severe illness in animals[4].

*Environmental effects*
Parathion residues may persist in the soil at high levels for up to five years, and at lower levels for up to 16 years. Highly hazardous to many types of domestic and wild animals and highly toxic to bees and fish. Parathion has been responsible for many of the illnesses and deaths from pesticide poisonings[1].
From 1992, parathion was banned in 17 countries and severely restricted in 3.

## Paraquat
*Acute effects*
Skin irritation and delays in healing of wounds[4]. Eye and skin irritant. Liver and kidney failure and failure of respiratory system. Damage to nails, coughing, vomiting, asthmatic attacks and inflamation of respiratory tract, scarred lungs and death[1].
*Chronic effects*
Linked with aplastic anaemia. Possible animal mutagen. Possible animal teratogen and embryotoxic. In animals causes weight loss, changes in lungs and mobility[4].
*Environmental effects*
Non-selective herbicide. One of the most toxic organic herbicides in animal systems. Moderately toxic to birds and aquatic invertebrates and slightly toxic to freshwater fish. Persistent in soil. Has significant adverse effects on certain stages of bird reproduction[1]. One of its degradation products, QINA chloride, does not bind well to soil and therefore is a potential groundwater contaminant[1]. There have been many human fatalities from accidental ingestion of concentrated paraquat liquid[4].
As at 1992 paraquat was banned in 6 countries and severely restricted in 2.

## Phosphine
*Acute Effects*
Sickness, stomach pain, vomiting and diarrhoea. Walking difficulties, convulsions, unconsciousness, death[3].
*Chronic effects*

No data.
*Environmental Effects*
No data.

## Picloram
*Acute effects*
Skin, eye and respiratory tract irritant[4].
*Chronic effects*
Possible animal carcinogen. Chronic renal disease[4].
*Environmental effects*
One of the most persistent herbicide in use in soil. Also very toxic to non-target plants. Harmful to fish[4].

## Propoxur
*Acute effects*
Cholinesterase inhibitor. Vomiting, cramps, diarrhoea, convulsions, confusions, exhaustion[4].
*Chronic effects*
Breakdown products are mutagenic and embryotoxic in animals. Effects on mammals' livers[4].
*Environmental effects*
One of the most persistent herbicide in use in soil. Also very toxic to non-target plants. Harmful to fish, livestock, game, wild birds, mammals and fish[4].

## Simazine
*Acute effects*
Skin and eye irritant. Irritating to respiratory system. Low toxicity[4].
*Chronic effects*
Weak animal mutagen and carcinogen. Neurotoxic and reproductive effects in animals[4].
*Environmental effects*
Low toxicity to fish[4]

## Zineb

*Acute effects*

Skin, eye and mucous membrane irritant. Allergies, headaches, vertigo, thirst, weakness, nausea and vomiting[4].

*Chronic effects*

Animal carcinogen and possible animal mutagen[4]. In animals inhibits growth. May affect blood and cause allergies. In humans affects liver, causes anaemia and affects reproductive system. Possible human carcinogen[2].

*Environmental effects*

Toxic to fish at certain levels. Harmful to poultry and game[4].

## 2,4,5 T

*Acute effects*

Burning of mouth and throats, stomach cramps, vomiting and diarrohea. Muscle weakness, confusion, coma. Skin irritation, nose bleeds, fatigue. Covulsions. Liver and kidney damage[1].

*Chronic effects*

Positive human carcinogen, teratogen and mutagen. Non-Hodgkins lymphoma. Soft tissue sarcoma[4].

*Environmental effects*

Very effective herbicide. Toxicity low to animals. Not persistent in soil. 2,4,5-T is persistent in the environment and toxic to wildlife, especially fish[4].

As at 1992, 2,4,5-T was banned in 31 countries and severely restricted in 2.

## 2,4 D

*Acute effects*

Positive human carcinogen, teratogen and mutagen.      Non-Hodgkins lymphoma. Soft tissue sarcoma[1].

*Chronic effects*

Burning of mouth, stomach cramps, vomiting and diarrohea. Muscle weakness, confusion, coma. Skin irritation, nosebleeds, fatigue. Covulsions. Liver and kidney damage. Dizziness[1].

*Environmental effects*
Very effective herbicide. Toxicity low to animals. Not persistent in soil.
2, 4 D is persistent in the environment and toxic to wildlife, especially fish[1].

\* These pesticides have been used on cocoa but are no longer produced. Stockpiles still exist.

## Sources

1. Pesticides Action Network International: Dirty Dozen Pesticides Fact Sheets Global Pesticides Campaigner vol 12 No 12
2. P is for Pesticides, Dr Tim Lang and Dr Charlie Clutterbuck, Ebury Press 1991
3. The Pesticide Handbook, Peter Hurst, Alastair Hay and Nigel Dudley, Journeyman 1991
4. Pesticide Users Health and Safety Handbook, Andrew Watterson, Gower Technical 1988

## Other Reading

This Poisoned Earth, Nigel Dudley, Piatkus 1987
The Use and Significance of Pesticides in the Environment. F L McEwen, G R Stephenson 1979.

# Appendix 2

## Company profiles of the five largest chocolate manufacturers

**Nestlé S.A**

Avenue Nestlé 55, CH 1800 Vevey, SWITZERLAND

Telephone Number in UK (021) 924 2111

Subsidiary Companies in the UK include  Nestlé-Rowntree P.O. Box 202, York, YO1 1XY.

Products: Nescafe, Carnation, Chambourcy,  and many more

International Operations: Global production, manufacturing and sales with manufacturing operations in 61 countries.

Employees 199,021 (group total)

Annual Turnover  US$36 511m (1990) Swiss Francs 46,369m

Profit Before Tax US$1,494m (1990) Sw F 4,656m[1]

One of the largest food companies in the world, Nestlé has reached its present position through a trail of expansion, acquisition and global-scale operations[2]. Sales in 1990 reached US$30 billion and trading profits of US$5 billion were derived from a large variety of drinks, foods and cosmetics of which chocolate and confectionery contributed around 15%[3]. As notorious for its baby milk as it is famous for its coffee, the company has provoked outrage for its baby milk marketing around the world. Since attention was first drawn to these activities in the early 1970's, a wide range of organisations worldwide have called for a boycott of Nestlé products.  In the UK these include hundreds of health, consumer, development, and church groups, student unions, and Members of Parliament.  The Church of England General Synod endorsed the boycott in July 1991[4] .

Nestlé began in business in the late 1800's making condensed milk  before teaming up with Swiss chocolate maker Daniel Peter to produce milk chocolate. Chocolate companies proliferated in Switzerland during the 1800's, from the first at Vevey in 1918, followed throughout the regions by names which are known today - Tobler, Cailler, Suchard, Lindt and others[5]. From the turn of the century Swiss chocolate developed a good reputation and Swiss consumption became so prolific that it began to exceed that of the Americans, Germans, French and English, reaching the top position they maintain today[6]. In 1990 the Swiss were still the largest consumers eating 8 .7 kilos of chocolate per person per year[7].

Nestlé expanded worldwide from its 15 factories in 1900 to over 400 in the 1990's as they diversified from milk and chocolate products to pasta and coffee[8]. As one of the biggest instant coffee sellers with a huge share of the £520 million business, they came under investigation by the Monopolies and Mergers Commission in March 1991,  although the outcome of a nine month enquiry indicated that the consumer was not disadvantaged by such a heavily monopolised position[9]. After engulfing Rowntrees in 1988, Nestlé became the largest chocolate manufacturer in the world[10]. The EC Commission was at that time reviewing movements within the confectionery industry in Europe, having witnessed Suchard takeover Belgian Cote D'Or for £73 million, Cadbury-Schweppes take over French Poulain for £95 million and Nestlé's previous takeover of Perugina. Nestlé's Rowntrees acquisition however did not come under the investigative gaze of the Monopolies and Mergers Commission, when The British Trade Secretary considered it unneccesary to refer the move[11]. Today Nestlé does business in 60 countries and, promoted by worldwide advertising and distribution, it makes the biggest confectionery sales the world over at $7.4 billion Swiss francs in 1990[12].

**Mars Inc**
6885 Elm Street, McLean, Virginia, 22101-3883 USA
UK Telephone Number 0753 550055
Products include: Mars Bar, Twix, Snickers, Bounty, Milky Way, Maltesers, Galaxy, Applause, Lockets, M&M's, Marathon.
Other Lines include petfood and pasta
International Operations: global sales operation
Employees 28,000
Annual Turnover around US$12 billion annually[13]

Established in Chicago, Forest E Mars began manufacturing confectionery in 1930 and now 50 years on manufacturers and sells around the world[14]. Until recent successsion by Nestlé, Mars claimed the largest volume of confectionery sales worldwide. The company today owns subsidiary manufacturing companies throughout Europe which take around 26% of the market[15] and contribute to worldwide sales of around US$12 billion. The company concentrates on manufacturing and sales.

**Jacobs Suchard**

Seefeld Quai No 17, P.O. Box 147, 8034 Zurich, SWITZERLAND
UK Telephone Number (071) 385 1111
Parent company: Philip Morris
Products include Suchard, Tobler, Milka, Cote d'Or, Jacobs, Brach
Other Lines: Coffee

International Operations Manufacturing and distribution throughout Europe and N America, and in Argentina. Import and distribution in Japan, Hong Kong, Taiwan, Singapore. Distribution in Australia. Licensees in Thailand, Malaysia, Indonesia, Singapore, Korea, Mexico, Portugal and South Africa.
Employees 16,000 group
Annual Turnover 6.6 billion SF (1989)
Profit Before Tax 373m SF (1989)[16]

This Swiss company predominating in world confectionery markets has expanded in a similar fashion from small family beginnings in the early 1800s[17]. And like Nestlé, this company is also heavily involved in coffee[18]. Jacobs Suchard steadily bought up companies throughout Europe since first annexing Tobler in the last century, but as throughout the rest of the industry, the biggest amalgamations have occurred in the last decade[19]. Since joining with Jacobs in 1982, Suchard bought four or five Belgium companies, including Cote D'Or, and increased sales in North America by buying an American company EJ Brach. In 1988, eager to increase their share of the UK market already worth £60 million they launched the takeover bid on Rowntree-

Mackintosh in 1988 only to lose out to rivals Nestlé[20]. With 13% of the European market and holding third place in the US following acquisiton of Brach, Jacobs Suchard recorded sales of 6.6 billion Swiss francs in 1989 and a trading profit of 372,000 Swiss francs[21]. In 1990 they themselves were taken over by the American food and tobacco giant Phillip Morris who paid £2.2 billion in order to place chocolate alongside their cigarettes and beer[22]. As a result of this takeover, a huge confectionery business was drawn into an even bigger conglomerate numbering among the top 200 US companies with sales of in 1990 of $51 billion[23].

**Hershey Foods Corporation**
P.O. Box 814, Hershey, PA 17033, USA
Subsidiary Companies include Delmonico Foods Div, Hershey Pasta GP, Ludens Div, San Giorgio-Skinner Co Div.
Products include Hershey bars, Hershey kisses, Reese's peanut butter cups,
Other Lines: Pasta
International Operations: Joint ventures in the Philippines, Mexico and Japan[24]. Owns a cocoa plantation in Belize[25].
Employees 12,700[26]
Annual Turnover  US$ 2,715 million (1990)
Net profit     US$   215 million (1990)[27]

The first confectionery company to set up in the US was established in Pensylvania in 1905 by Milton S Hershey who built what is now the largest confectionery production plant. Familiar with confectionery manufacturing technology he established the most technologically advanced plant of the time and began mass production[28]. With sales now around $2.7 billion in 1990 and a net income of $215,000, Hershey bars are one of the best selling bars in the US today. Whilst it has some licensing agreements to sell abroad, Hershey unlike the other major confectionery companies sells mainly to the domestic American market[29].

**Cadbury Schweppes PLC**
1-4 Connaught Place, London W2
UK Telephone Number (071) 262 1212
Products include Dairy Milk, Roses, Twirl, Crunchie, Milk Tray, Creme Eggs
Wispa, Fruit & Nut, Flake, Whole Nut, Caramel.
Other Lines: Fizzy Drinks
International Operations: Exports to 110 countries
Manufactures in 15 countries. Major presence in US, Eire, S Africa, Australia,
New Zealand, India and Malaysia
Employees  35,653 (1990 worldwide)
Annual Turnover  £3,146.1m (1990)
Profit Before Tax  £279.6m (1990)
Marketing Budget  £324.7 m (1990)30

Cadbury was established in the early 1800's  as were a number of other family firms including Rowntree, Fry and Terry. Promoted by the Cadbury brothers import of the Dutch invented cocoa press in 1866, chocolate consumption became affordable and accessible for many people and the business flourished.  Like the other British companies, they expanded production around the world between the wars setting up subsidiary operations in the Commonwealth and colonies, in Australia, New Zealand and South Africa, and in India after Independence. Since World War2 and the dissolution of the colonies, Cadbury have built factories in the producer countries of Nigeria, Ghana, and Malaysia[31]. Cadbury merged with Schweppes in 1969 and Cadbury-Schweppes is now one of the biggest companies in Britain with annual sales of over £3 billion in 1990. The British confectionery market is the largest in Europe, worth £3.7 billion in 1990 71% of which is chocolate[32].. By 1989 Cadbury had cornered 29% of this including five of the top ten brands worth £300 million[33].  As well as importing semimanufactured products from the Netherlands, they also process beans at a plant in Wales to supply their Birmingham manufacturing plant[34].

*References*

Nestlé

1. Nestlé Annual Report 1990, p 3.

2. ibid Annual Report 1990, p 6-8.

3. ibid Annual Report 1990, p 22.

4. Baby Milk Action factsheet, available from Campaign Against Nestlé, BMAC, Cambridge. January 1993.

5. Chocologie: or chocology: a concise vade mecum through the Chocolate Industry in Switzerland. Published by the Union of Swiss Chocolate Manufacturers, Munzgraben 6, 3000 Bern 7. Page 22-23.

6. ibid Chocologie, p 24.

7. See table in chapter 2.

8. ibid Annual Report 1990, p 22.

9. Financial Times, 9 March 1991.

10. Financial Times 24 June 1988

11. Financial Times, 3 May 1988.

12. ibid Annual Report 1990, p 22.

Mars

13. Independent on Sunday, 26 July 1992.

14. Independent on Sunday, 26 July 1992.

15. Financial Times, 30 September 1992.

Jacobs Suchard

16. Annual Report 1989, p 1.

17. Chocologie, p 20-21.

18. Annual Report 1989, p15.

19. See chapter 8 on profit.

20. Financial Times, 24 June 1988.

21. Annual Report 1989, p 1.

22. Keynote Confectionery Report.

23. Philip Morris Companies Inc. Annual Report 1990, p 1.

Hershey

24. A Tradition of Excellence, published by Hershey, p11.

25. Coffee and Cocoa International, issue 4, 1984.

26. Six-Year Consolidated Financial Summary.

27. Six-Year Consolidated Financial Summary.

28. Tradition, p 1-3.

29. Tradition, p 11.

Cadbury

30. Annual Report 1990, p 2-3.

31. "Multinational Chocolate: Cadbury Overseas, 1918-1939" by Geoffrey Jones in Business History, vol. 26, number 1, March 1984, p 59-74.

32 A market sector overview : Confectioney, Keynote report 1991

33 Sweet Facts of 1990, Rowntree-Nestlé 1990.

34 Report of Chocolate Conference, Schloss Gnadenthal, West Germany 23-26th January 1989, TIE; Amsterdam 1989.

# Tables

**Table 1** UK RETAIL SALES OF CONFECTIONERY 1985-91

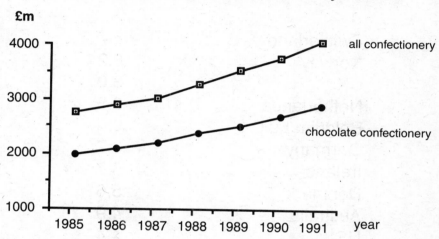

**U.K. Retail Sales of Confectionery 1985-91**

Sources: BCCA Annual Review (1991); Market Assessment (1990)

**Table 2** CHOCOLATE CONSUMPTION PER CAPITA

# CHOCOLATE CONSUMPTION
# (KG/CAPITA/YEAR)

| | |
|---|---|
| Switzerland | 8.7 |
| Norway | 8.2 |
| UK | 8.0 |
| Netherlands | 6.8 |
| Belguim/Lux | 6.8 |
| Germany | 6.7 |
| Ireland | 5.7 |
| Denmark | 5.6 |
| Australia | 4.9 |
| US | 4.4 |
| France | 4.2 |
| Italy | 4.1 |

*Source: Keynote report - A Market Sector Overview,*
*Confectionery 1991*

**Table 3** MEDIA SPEND ON ADVERTISING

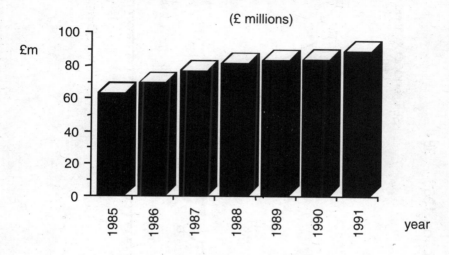

## Main Media Spend on Advertising
## Chocolate Confectionery 1985-91

(£ millions)

£m

Sorces: Meal Assessment (1990); Mintel (1992)

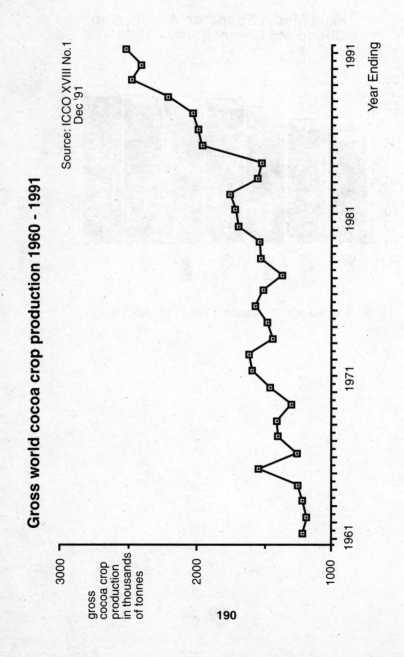

Gross world cocoa crop production 1960 - 1991

Source: ICCO XVIII No.1
Dec '91

**Table 5** TOP 12 COCOA BEAN PRODUCERS

## Top 12 Cocoa Bean Producers 1989-1990

| | |
|---|---|
| World Total | 2,379,200 |
| Ivory Coast | 714,000 |
| Brazil | 347,900 |
| Ghana | 295,100 |
| Malaysia | 243,000 |
| Nigeria | 160,000 |
| Cameroon | 125,700 |
| Indonesia | 115,000 |
| Ecuador | 95,200 |
| Dominican Republic | 58,000 |
| Colombia | 50,000 |
| Mexico | 43,000 |
| Papua New Guinea | 40,800 |

*Source: ICCO XV11 No. 4 Sept 1991*

**Table 6** AVERAGE DAILY COCOA PRICE

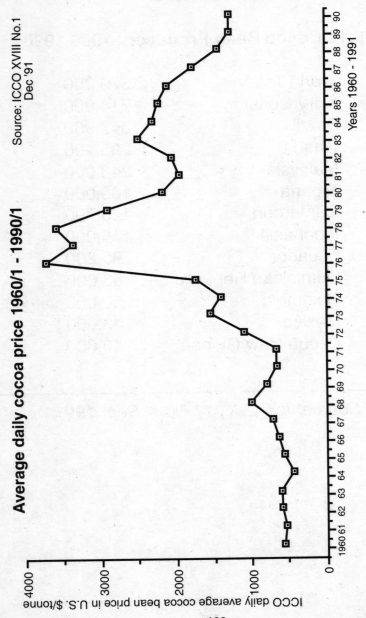

Source: ICCO XVIII No.1
Dec '91

Average daily cocoa price 1960/1 - 1990/1

ICCO daily average cocoa bean price in U.S. $/tonne

Years 1960 - 1991

**Table 7** UK CONFECTIONERY MARKET

# Share of UK Confectionery Market 1992

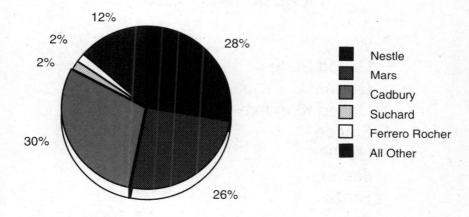

Source: Financial Times 30/9/92

# Top 12 Cocoa Final Consumers by Country
# in tonnes, 1989 - 1990

| | |
|---|---|
| World Total | 2,079,000 |
| United States | 562,000 |
| Germany | 253,600 |
| United Kingdom | 162,100 |
| France | 146,200 |
| USSR | 134,200 |
| Japan | 109,500 |
| Brazil | 74,100 |
| Italy | 68,700 |
| Spain | 52,000 |
| Canada | 51,000 |
| Belguim/Lux | 47,200 |
| Colombia | 39,200 |

*Source ICCO XV111 No. 1 Dec 1991*

# Contact Addresses

Action and Information on Sugars
28 St Pauls Street
London N1 7AB

Christian Aid
PO Box 100 SE1 7RT

Green and Black Chocolate
Whole Earth Foods Ltd
269 Portobello Road
London W11 1LR

Health Education Authority
Hamilton House
Mabledon Place
London WC1H 9TX

Hyperactive Children's Support Group
71 Whyke Lane
Chichester
Sussex PO1 92LD

London Food Commission
5-11 Worship Rd
London EC2A 2BH

Natonal Food Alliance
5-11 Worship Rd
London EC2A 2BH

Max Havelaar
PO Box 1252
3500 BG Utrecht
Netherlands

Parents for Safe Food
c/o National Food Alliance
5-11 Worship Rd
London EC2A 2BH

Pesticides Trust
23 Beehive Place
Brixton SW9 7QR

SAFE Alliance
21 Tower St
London WC2H 9NS

Soil Association
86 Colston Street
Bristol BS1 5BB

SOMO
132 Kaisergracht
1015 CW Amsterdam
Netherlands

Traidcraft
Kingsway
Gateshead
Tyne and Wear NE11 0NE

Transnational Information Exchange
Paulus Potterstreet 20
1071 DA Amsterdam
Netherlands

Twin Trading
5-11 Worship Rd
London EC2A 2BH

Women's Environmental Network
Aberdeen Studios
22 Highbury Grove
London N5 2EA

Women's Therapy Centre
6 Manor Gardens
London N7 6LA

World Development Movement
25 Beehive Place
London SW9 7QR

# Index

Acceptable Daily Intake (ADI) 47
Additives 37-9
        health effects 39-40
Advertising campaigns 25
Advertising myths 25
Agrochemical use increase 139
Agrochemical in food 55
Agrochemicals see also Pesticides
Alar 53
Aldicarb 110(fig.)
Aldrin 110(fig.)
        as carcinogen 97
        in cocoa 56(fig.)
American Cocoa Research Institute 128
Ames, Professor Bruce 51
Animal toxicity tests 50
Anorexia 30
Aphrodisiac significance 20
Arsenic 96
Arumugam, Vasanthi 101
Asthma and additives 39
Atkinson, Paul 21
Atrazine-tolerant canola 130
Automated wrapping and boxing 36
Aztecs cocoa use 12

Baby food, dye bans 40
Barthes, Roland 21
Bayer 105
Beauty and guilt 31-2
Binge food 28
Binging 29-31
Biotechnology 126-37
        dangers 132
        effects on producers 133-4
Biscuit, Cake, Chocolate and
Confectionery Alliance (BCCCA),
        pesticide residue testing 48-9
Black pod disease 100
Bloom prevention 36

Bolivia, cooperative cocoa groups141-2
Borneo see Kalimantan
Brazil,
        cocoa bean
        destinations 94 (fig.)
        cocoa butter
        destinations 94 (fig.)
        cocoa cultivation 71-6
        cocoa export 73
        industrial development 72-3
        pesticide use 103
        working conditions 73-4
Brewster, Havelock 116
British Commonwealth Development
Corporation 91
Bromoxynil-resistant cotton 130
Brown, Lester 130
Bulimia 30
Bunday, Sally 39

Cacao Barry 117
Cadbury Flake advertisement 21
Cadbury-Schweppes 13-14, 42, 119
        expansion 120
        profits 119
        R & D projects 134
Caffeine 23-4
Camphechlor 110 (fig.)
Cancer, and pesticide exposure 98
Cannon, Geoffrey 42-3
CAOBISCO 37-8
Carbaryl poisoning 102
Carcinogenicity in additives 39
Cargill 114, 117
Carrots, resistant 130
Carson, Rachel 98, 108, 143
Cash crops, dependence reduction
144-5
CEPLAC 103
Chemical production, toxicity 106-7
Chemicals,
        and the body 23-4
        in food 40

Children, susceptibility
  to toxic chemicals 53
Chlordane 110 (fig.)
Chlordimeform 110 (fig.)
Chocoholic confessions 26-7
Chocolate,
  British weekly consumption 19
  chemical constituents 23-4
  ingredients 34-7
  as luxury 19
  mass consumption 14
  as 'problem' food 39
  processing industry 116-17
  residue safety level 50
  as romantic food 18-23
  symbolic significance 15, 18
Chocolate boxes,
  Cadbury decoration in 1868 22
  as romantic gifts 21-2
  springtime purchase 23
Chocolate industry and cocoa chain
changes 145
Chocolate Manufacturers' Association 55
Chocolate packaging 22-3
Chocolate see also Cocoa
Chocolate 12, 20
Circle of Poison 54-5
Cocoa,
  agreements 115-16
  diseases 100
  genetic engineering 129
  as Ghanaian quality product 63-4
  hardship for growers 140
  introduction to Malaysia 79
  mass production 16
  as Mayan fertility symbol 10
  for organic chocolate 142
  organic production 145
  pesticide residues in 56 (fig.)
  pesticides 100-101
  price rise 37
  prices 114
  as prosperity symbol 11
  and sacred rites 10-12

  and sacred rites 10-12
  stocks 115
  supply and demand 113
  trade 112-3
Cocoa beans 10
  as currency 11
  genetic improvement 128
  introduction to West Africa 61
  Mayan beverage 11
  pesticide residues 48-9
  top destinations 94 (fig.)
Cocoa butter 35
  laboratory creation 128, 135-6
  substitution 134-5
  top destinations 94 (fig.)
Cocoa Butter Equivalents (CBEs) 37
Cocoa Butter Improvers (CBIs) 37
Cocoa cake 35
Cocoa de Zaan 49
Cocoa farmers, unrewarded 64-5
Cocoa mass, pretreatment 36
Cocoa nib 34
Cocoa pod borers 105
Cocoa powder 13
Cocoa see also Chocolate
Cocoa tree 10
  growth 58-9
  hybrids in Malaysia 132
  insect damage 100
  manipulation 131-3
  species 58
  yield increase 128
Cocoa Tree chocolate house 13
Cocobod 64, 66, 100
  pesticide practice 104-5
Codex Committee on Pesticide Residues
(CCPR) 47
Collins, J. 68
COMA report, 1991 42-3
Committee on Medical
  Aspects of Food Policy 42
Commodity prices, comparison 122 (fig.)
Commodity trading 113-115

Compulsive eating 29-30
Conching 36
Cornell University 136
Cortez and cocoa 12
Coward, Rosalind 20-1
Criollo tree 58
Culpepper, Complete Herbal 20

DBCP 110 (fig.)
DDE, residue in food 54
DDT 96, 104, 110 (fig.)
        in cocoa 56 (fig.)
        US ban 108
Deforestation,
        in Indonesia 92
        in Peninsula Malaysia 83
Delaney Clause 52
Diaz, B., The Conquest of New Spain 20
Dichlorvos 44
        in cocoa 56 (fig.)
        and developing nervous
        system 53
Dieldrin 110 (fig.)
        as carcinogen 97
        in cocoa 56 (fig.)
Diet related diseases, mortality 42
Dieting 29-31
Dioxin toxicity 107
Dirty Dozen list 54, 100, 102, 108, 110
(fig.)
Diseases linked to sugar 41
DNA modification 129
Dow Chemicals 130
Du Barry, Madame,
        as chocolate drinker 20

E is for Additives 39
Easter and chocolate industry 15
Easter eggs 15
Eating disorders 30
EC directive on additive labelling 39
EC lindane level in cocoa 49
EC regulations 37
Ecofeminists 146

Ecologist 92
Economic instability through
        biotechnology 137
Ecosystem and pesticides 98
EDB 110 (fig.)
El Ceibo 141
Elshof, Paul 118
Endorphins 24
Endosulfan 103
Endrin 110 (fig.)
        in cocoa 56 (fig.)
Environmental perspectives 146
Environmental Protection Agency
        (EPA) 51
        pesticide residue levels 52
Enzyme techniques 135
Epstein, Professor Samuel 52
Ethical consumption 143
Ethyl vanillin 40
European influences, early 12-13
European market by company 123 (fig.)

Fair trade 140-2
Fat,
        consumption reduction 43
        role in breast cancer 52
        in UK diet 40, 42,3
Feingold Diet 39
FELDA 84, 118
Ferrero Rocher,
        Baci 23
        packaging 22
Fertilisers 99
Flavourings addition 36
Food,
        contamination by pesticides 97
        and sex connection 20-1
        symbolic appeal 21
Food & Agricultural Organisation
        (FAO) 47
Food and Drink Federation 42
Food First in 1980 68
Food Magazine 44
Food pornography 20-1

Food processing 135
Food testing 45-9
Forastero tree 58
Friends of the Earth Malaysia 91, 103
Fritz, Dr P.J . 128, 131
Fruit and nut addition 36
Fuji Oil Company 134
Fungicides 10

Garotto chocolate factory 74
GATT(General Agreement on Tariffs and Trade) 144
Gender in chocolate 25
Genencor 134
Genetic modification 126-7
     safety considerations 127
Ghana ,
     cocoa bean destinations 94 (fig.)
     cocoa butter destinations 94 (fig.)
     cocoa as cash crop 61-3
     cocoa export and debt 68
     Cocoa Marketing Board 64
     economic regeneration 65-6
     pesticide use 104-5
     political and economic changes 64-5
     social implications 67
Gill and Duffis 114-15
Global economic system trends 140
Glyphosphate resistance 129
Grace, W R 117
Green Consumer 143
Greenpeace 106-7
Guthrie 83

Health Education Authority (HEA) 41-3
Heptachlor 110 (fig.)
Heptachlor, in cocoa 56 (fig.)
Herbicide resistance 130
Hershey, Milton 14
Hershey bars 14
Hershey Foods,
     and cocoa butter by tissue

culture 136
    cocoa clone production patent application 132
    investment in Belize 118
    in Malaysia 119
    profits 119
Hexachlorobenzene, in cocoa 56 (fig.)
Honey as aphrodisiac 20
Hot chocolate 13
Houhpouet-Boigny, Felix 115
House of Commons Committee on Pesticides and Health 50
Hyperactive Children's Support Group 39

ICCO 112,115
Independent Television Commission, complaints to 31
India, DDT ban 108
Indonesia,
    cocoa production 89-93
    plantation development 90-1
    threat to diversity 91-3
    transmigration 89-90
Inorganic bromide, in cocoa 56 (fig.)
Inquinosa 106
Insecticides for cotton 100
International Cocoa Organisation 112, 115
International Monetary Fund (IMF) 65, 68, 116, 140
Intolerable Risk: pesticides in our children's food 53
Irian Jaya 89-91
Irradiation, effects on food residues 51
Israel, breast cancer reduction 52
Ivory Coast,
    cocoa bean destinations94(fig.)
    cocoa butter destinations94 (fig.)
Ixcacao 10
Japan,
    chocolate consumption 120-1

chocolate purchase 23
Java 90
Joanes S. A. 76

Kalimantan 89-90
Kit Kat 14, 25, 120

Land erosion 99
Lappe, Frances M. 68
Lethicin 36
Lindane 44, 46, 104, 110 (fig.)
    banning and restriction 54
    as carcinogen 97-8
    in cocoa 56 (fig.)
    in cocoa beans 48-9
    as food residue 54
    in Ghana 105-6
    persistent toxicity 106
    restriction by countries 111 (fig.)
    restriction by EPA 106
    sprayers' symptoms 110 (fig.)
    as teratogen 54
Lindt boxed chocolates 22
Liquor 34-5

Maize, sugar substitutes from 135
Malaysia,
    cocoa bean destinations 94 (fig.)
    cocoa butter destinations 94 (fig.)
    cocoa as cash crop 79, 83
    cocoa cultivation 79-86
    economic expansion 82
    Era of Cocoa Developement 83
    increased cocoa yields 132
    `nucleus estate plantation` 84, 90
    `opening up the land` policy 82-4
    paraquat use 102
    pesticide use 101-2
    plantation life 79-82
    plantation productivity 83
    resettlement into cash
    economy 84-6
Maldevelopment 69
Mancozeb 103

Mann, E.D. & F. 76, 114-15
Manufacturers, concentration 118-20
Maria Theresa, Princess of Spain 22
Mars, Forest E. 14
Mars bars 14
    additives 38
Mars Inc.,
    in China 121
    in Malaysia 119
    profits 119
Max Havelaar Foundation 141
Maximum Residue Levels (MRL) 47-9
Mayans, sacred cocoa 10-11
Meat and men`s control over
    women 18-19
Mentawai people 92
Mexico, cocoa beans as currency 11
Milk chocolate, manufacture 35
Ministry of Agriculture, Food and
Fisheries (MFF) ,
    dye bans 39-40
    Working Party on Pesticide
    Residues 53
Mintel 143
Mirids, lindane-resistant 104
Models, weight drop 31
Monoculture 98-100
Monsanto 129
Moon-hare 15
Mouth-feel of chocolate 23, 36

Natural Resources Defense Council
(NRDC) 53
Nestlé-Rowntree 14, 25, 47, 118-119
    in Brazil 76
    in Malaysia 121
    market share 120
New World Order 144
Newly industrialised countries (NICs) 82

Orbach, Susie 29
Organic cultivation 142-4
Organochlorines 96
Organophosphates 96

Packaging, resource waste 22-3
Palm-oil 37
PAMSCAD 67
Paraquat 110 (fig. )
    In Brazil 103
    poisoning 102-3
    sprayers' symptoms 111(fig.)
    US safety recommendations 102
Parathion 96, 110 (fig.)
Pennsylvania State project 131-2
Pennsylvania State University 128-9
Pentachlorophenol 110 (fig.)
Pest control 143
Pesticide Action Network 48, 54, 100, 108, 110 (fig.)
Pesticide poisoning, symptoms 101-2
Pesticide trade 107-9
Pesticide workers, health effects 97
Pesticide-resistant crops 130
Pesticides 96-111
    acceptable daily intake (ADI) 50
    and children 52-4
    chronic health effects 97
    in fat 52
    human carcinogenic potential 50
    levels in food 46
    long term effects 51
    pre-packaged 44-5
    production dangers 106-7
    residues found in cocoa 56 (fig.)
Pesticides see also Agrochemicals; Residues
Phenylethylamine 24
Philip Morris 119
Phillip Brothers 116
Plantation agriculture promotion 138
Plantation economy in Brazil 71
Prior Informed Consent (PIC) 108
Proctor and Gamble 25
Programme of Action to Mitigate the Social Consequences of Adjustment 67
Propoxur 104-5

    in cocoa 56 (fig.)
Pyrethrins 96

Quinoline Yellow 38-9

Rawlings, Jerry 65
Residues
    acceptable doses 49-52
    body intakes 49-52
    in chocolate 44-9
    cumulative effect 53-4
    possible synergistic reaction 54
    testing 45-9
    unknown effects on children 53
Residues see also Pesticides
Resistance, creation of in-built 129
Rhiannon 14
Rhone Poulenc 130
Roundup 129
Royal Commission on Environmental Pollution 131

Sabah, cocoa crop 83-4
Sahabat Alam Malaysia 81, 103
Sarawak, cocoa cultivation 84
Self-sufficiency renewal 14
Sexual images 18-23
Shiva, Vandana 69
Siberut 92
Silent Sprint 98, 108, 143
Sime Darby 83
    plantations 119
Skin reactions to additivies 39
Slimming business 30
Soil depletion 99
SOMO 118
Sorbitan stearates 38
Stanley, Dr 46
Sterilization certificate for employment in Brazil 75
Structural adjustment programmes (SAPs) 65, 68

Stubbe, Dr The Indian Nectar of a
Discourse Concerning Cocoa 23
Suchard, J. 47, 119, 121
Sucres et Denrees 114, 116
Sugar,
    addiction 24
    in UK diet 40-3
Sugar Bureau 42
Suicide by pesticide 101
Sulphur 96
Sumatra 89
Synergistic effects of chemicals 54

Tamils in Malaysia 79
Targeting of women 25
Television, chocolate advertising 18
Tempering 36
Thaumatiin 131
Theobroma cacao, molecular biology
investigation 128
Theobromine 23-4
Third World debt 67-9
Tobacco, 2, 4-D-resistant 130
Tooth decay and sugar 41
Total Diet Study 45-6, 48
Trading patterns 117
Traidcraft 141
Transnational companies 118
    in Brazil 75-6

Transnational Information Exchange (TIE)
75-6
Trinitario tree 58
Tropical chocolate 38, 121
Tuke, Mary 14
Twin Trading 141

UK,
    advertising spending 25
    confectionery market 14
    heart disease rate 42
    labelling regulations 37
    pesticide registration 51

pesticide residue level
    regulations 47
UK Committee on Toxicology of
Chemicals in the Environment 53
UK Department of Health, Committee on
Toxicity 53
UN Codex Committee on Pesticide
Residues 47
UN Conference on Trade and
Development (UNCTAD) 114, 116
UN Food and Agriculture Organisation,
Code of Conduct on pesticides 108
UNESCO Biosphere Reserve 92
Unilever 25, 134-5
Union Carbide 130
United Plantations 83
US Chocolate Manufacturers'
        Association 128
US confectionery market 14
US Farm Bill 'Circle of Poison'
Amendment 5
US National Academy of Sciences 51-2

Van Houten 13
Vanilla, laboratory production 136
Vanilla farmers, future prospects 136
Vegetable fats, added 37
Victims without Voice 101

Weed control by paraquat 102
Weight control 30
West Africa, cocoa cultivation 61-9
Wispa bars 14
    automated production 37

Witches' broom disease 100
Wolf, N., The Beauty Myth 30
Women,
    as chocolate
    consumers 14, 21-2
    in Ghanaian cocoa culture 62-3

on Malaysian plantations 80-2
oppression in Brazil 74-5
as pesticide sprayers 101-2
relationship with food 28-9
resettlement in Sarawak 85
Working Party on Pesticide Residues 46
World Bank 65-6, 68, 82, 140, 143
and pesticide approval 104
pesticide policy hesitation 106
World Health Organisation 42
agrochemical poisoning
estimate 97-8
World Watch Institute 130